STAINED GLASS HEARTS

Also by Patsy Clairmont

*Kaleidoscope: Seeing God's Wit and Wisdom
in a Whole New Light*

I Second That Emotion: Untangling Our Zany Feelings

Dancing Bones: Living Lively in the Valley

All Cracked Up: Experiencing God in the Broken Places

I Grew Up Little: Finding Hope in a Big God

The Hat Box: Putting on the Mind of Christ

The Shoe Box: Walking in the Spirit

I Love Being a Woman

*5 Cheesy Stories: About Friendship, Bravery,
Bullying, and More*

STAINED GLASS HEARTS

Seeing Life from a Broken Perspective

PATSY CLAIRMONT

THOMAS NELSON
Since 1798

NASHVILLE   DALLAS   MEXICO CITY   RIO DE JANEIRO

Published in Nashville, Tennessee, by Thomas Nelson. Thomas Nelson is a registered trademark of Thomas Nelson, Inc.

Published in association with Books & Such Literary Agency, Janet Kobobel Grant, 52 Mission Circle, Suite 122, PMB 170, Santa Rosa, CA 95409.

Thomas Nelson, Inc., titles may be purchased in bulk for educational, business, fund-raising, or sales promotional use. For information, please e-mail SpecialMarkets@ ThomasNelson.com.

Unless otherwise noted, Scripture quotations are taken from the New American Standard Bible®, © The Lockman Foundation 1960, 1962, 1963, 1968, 1971, 1972, 1973, 1975, 1977, 1995. Used by permission.

Scripture quotations marked NKJV are from the New King James Version®. © 1982 by Thomas Nelson, Inc. Used by permission. All rights reserved.

Scripture quotations marked NIV are from the Holy Bible, New International Version®, NIV®. © 1973, 1978, 1984, 2011 by Biblica, Inc.™ Used by permission of Zondervan. All rights reserved worldwide. www.zondervan.com.

Scripture quotations marked KJV are from the King James Version.

Scripture quotations marked MSG are from the *The Message* by Eugene H. Peterson. © 1993, 1994, 1995, 1996, 2000, 2002. Used by permission of NavPress Publishing Group. All rights reserved.

Library of Congress Cataloging-in-Publication Data

Clairmont, Patsy.
  Stained glass hearts : seeing life from a broken perspective / Patsy Clairmont.
    p. cm.
  ISBN 978-0-8499-4826-8 (hardcover)
  1. Consolation. 2. Suffering—Religious aspects—Christianity. 3. Grace (Theology) I. Title.
  BV4905.3.C53 2011
  248.8'6—dc23   2011019013

Printed in the United States of America

12 13 14 15 QGF 6 5 4

To Mary Graham and my Porch Sisters,
who came to the rescue when my heart
broke into a thousand pieces:
my undying gratitude—
also to Jan Silvious,
who knows what to do for the hurting . . .
and tenderly did it.
Your friendships have taught me much about a
Stained Glass Perspective.

Contents

Chapter 1

The Heart
of the Matter

My grandson Noah, who is seven and in the second grade, is hesitant this year to enter the school day with a full heart. With regularity at night he says to his mom, "How 'bout I don't go to school tomorrow?"

That's the sweetest way I've ever heard of saying, "With your permission . . . I quit."

It isn't that Noah doesn't like school, his teacher, or his classmates. On the contrary, he is quite the ambassador of goodwill. But Noah finds school seriously eats into his playtime. It cramps his exuberant style. C'mon, it interferes with him romping with Sammie, his puppy.

I so get Noah's perspective. My life responsibilities mess with my dreams of an extended rocking chair retreat. I travel most weekends of the year to do conferences, which is both a joy and a pain. The pain is packing. I must have missed that class in high school home economics because I'm really poor at it, even after thirty-five years of perpetual travel.

On the night before a trip, I often want to say, "How 'bout I don't go to the airport tomorrow? How 'bout I just stay home?"

Yet here's what I know about me: after a few months of tipping lemonade on the front stoop, I would be saying, "How 'bout I go somewhere?"

I'm so grateful for a light-bearing Savior who came to redeem me from my self-absorbed viewpoints and my broken-glass perspective, lest I give in to my childish whims and miss my calling, my potential, and the opportunity to make legacy-bearing contributions.

This is my third book dedicated to the topic of light and redemption—two topics wed by God's benediction over creation in Genesis that continue to intrigue and inspire me. Two topics that can elevate us to a Pikes Peak perspective. Two topics that fill stained glass windows around the world with timeless inspiration. And two topics that move us past the temptation to quit before we have finished "school."

What might surprise you in this tome, however, is the timbre. I'm known for my playful approach to life, which is fused within me; but to those who are closest to me, I'm also known for my need to pull on galoshes and wade into a thought. I guess when you've lived sixty-plus years you collect a lot of heartache from this wind-whipped world that causes you to search the shadows of the forest. In my childhood I would have skipped through the woods oblivious to anything more than the path ahead, but today I've learned to check the secret places for the treasures of darkness (Isaiah 45:3).

This book, more than my past writings, reveals the solemn side of my heart etched in by loss. But I also plan to explore fascinating art that will potentially enrich our minds. We will enjoy music that hopefully inspires a zippier life-dance; we will consider nature's display of God's glory; and we will dig into Scripture, knowing it will enhance faith. Of course my funny bone is still intact, and if you know me, there's no telling when I might act up.

And no, I'm not an art major, a dance instructor, a conservationist, or a theologian. I'm a bona fide, card-carrying cracked pot, grateful that it pleases God to make himself known to us all . . . which brings us back around to redemption and light.

Light thrills me with its unexpected twists and turns as it bathes distant peaks and then plunges to the valley, illuminating paths below. As I pen these thoughts, I'm in a rocking chair on a Tennessee hilltop, watching the sunlight gyrate through the tops of thousands of acres of trees. It's like a living stained glass window where, for a weekend, I get to view amazing displays of God's handiwork.

Just as light does, redemption brings hope. Really, it's hard to separate the two, for wherever redemption is, the light of revelation abounds. And when light pierces the darkness, it's with the proclamation of God's redeeming love. Redemption is the rescue of humanity from sin by a sacrificial Savior, the restoration of the human heart, the reclamation of our dignity, and the revival of our purpose.

Oh, wait. Like a New York yellow cab at rush hour, a sun-drenched finch just dashed into the thickets below, staining the sky with its golden streak. Breathtaking. I like it here. A lot. I've been on this hilltop before but never long enough. Whenever I arrive here, my blood pressure drops, my stress level evens out, my spirits buoy, and I rest deeply in this hand-hewn cedar-and-cypress cabin. Because of the generosity of our friends Nordick and Mary Claire, I can step out of town and sit above the clouds—or sometimes smack-dab in the middle of them. It's a perfect perch from which to share with you my current events as well as those from times long ago.

When as a child I did something outlandish, my dad would quip that I had a "paper head." Funny thing, he never mentioned my stained glass heart. I wonder if he knew then how easily we shatter? I'm certain he was familiar with brokenness since he grew up in the Depression, when times were tough and people desperate. I'm not sure Dad absorbed the chaos of those years with its hardship since most of his life he remained an easygoing man who loved poker, naps, crossword puzzles, toothpicks, and the Charleston.

That is until my brother, Don, Dad's only son, died in a car accident and knocked the dance out of Daddy. I saw his heart shatter. When word came out of the operating room that there was no hope for Don, I found Dad alone, leaning against a wall in the hospital. He was clutching his chest as if he were trying to catch pieces of his heart as it broke. I took Dad outside, and when his color improved, we took him home to mend. That was one day of many to come when I was reminded that all God's people have glass hearts. Even dads. We aren't alone in our fragile design.

So come on into my storybook. Look around. Yes, I know it's personal, but you have my permission to ruffle the pages. While you're here, I'll share my tattered life with its crashes and recoveries because I believe in community wellness; we each contribute to others by sharing our successes and most certainly our failures. I believe we help each other know a fuller picture of Christ through the drama of what's happened to us and how he goes about daily redemption. I will also talk about the new vision and eventual version of us that comes with holy rescue. And I would like to chat about our stained hearts and our limited—as well as our expansive—perspectives that color who we are and how we relate to others.

First, though, I want to take you back to a miracle moment in the vortex of my once-suffocating existence . . .

For a long time I believed that if I just tried a little harder, I could fix my broken self, but no matter how thoroughly I rifled through my bag of tricks, I didn't have the tools recovery required. Then I bought into the lie that if I could redesign my life to circumvent my fears, I would make it through this scary maze called life. Only my fears multiplied, further constricting my ability to function. It seemed the more I adjusted my life to avoid what scared me, the more tightly fear coiled and hissed venomously.

Finally I gave up trying to reason my way out of my fear-based lifestyle and instead waited for a Clark Kent intervention. Then one morning I woke to the startling realization that I wasn't going to survive my agoraphobic self, much less the world, and that no cape-clad superhero had been assigned to my case.

I had, over several years, become emotionally and physically housebound; then I became bedbound and drug dependent, and my physical health was precarious at best. My weight had dropped to eighty-five pounds, and I was strung out on caffeine, nicotine, and heavy doses of fear. I popped tranquilizers like kids gobbled jawbreakers, trying to escape the darkness and panic that had seized my mind.

So what life-altering event caused a shaft of light to finally enter my debilitating gloom and bring me a glimmer of hope? Did I invite Christ into my heart? Actually, I already had done that. Unfortunately I filtered Scripture through my twisted thinking, which at best left me with a distorted picture of who God was. I read of God's judgment, and that aspect of him Velcroed to my overdeveloped guilt, but his words and acts of grace slipped through the cavernous hole in my heart. Grace was, in my thinking, reserved for someone more deserving, like the Abigails and Ruths of the Old Testament.

Did an angel finally appear and touch my bruised mind and restore my ragged health? Nope. I would have been thrilled with that kind of divine Jiffy Lube quick start. I was an eager advocate for fast, easy, and convenient restoration.

No, nary a flapping wing nor a fiery chariot arrived at my bedside to liberate me. Instead the turnaround came on a day when three simple yet startling words rose up inside of me and flashed like a neon arrow.

Before I tell you those life-changing words, though, I would like to talk about Chihuly. How random is that?

Have you heard of Dale Chihuly? Dale is a glass artist. In 1976 he was in a serious automobile accident that threw him through the car's windshield, causing him to lose his left eye. Vision is an important part of an artist's ability to maintain balance in his art and scope.

Then Dale injured his shoulder scuba diving, and those combined accidents forced him to step down from his coveted master glass grinder position. It appeared Chihuly's career in the art of glass would be greatly altered or perhaps even be over, but then a life-changing moment occurred. Listen to Dale in his own words . . .

"Once I stepped back [*okay, get ready, here it comes*], I enjoyed the view," said Chihuly. Did you hear that? "I. Enjoyed. The. View." He lost his vision in one eye, he lost his esteemed position, and he likes what he sees?

What he saw was his art from a new angle. His unwanted change gave him a different perspective. Dale couldn't have imagined that his limitations would position him to see limitless possibilities. He is now considered by many to be the premiere glass designer in the world. Chihuly's light-bearing work is displayed in hotels, castles, gardens, and museums throughout the world.

"Once I stepped back, I enjoyed the view." *Selah* (Hebrew for "Ponder this thought").

Now, return with me to my story and my breakthrough

moment. The three words that pushed their way through my cloying fear, bleak melancholy, and blinding stuck-ness were (*drums, please*) "Make your bed."

Yep. Not "Change the world," not "Go forth and conquer," but "Make your bed."

I pressed myself that day to respond, and I made the bed that I had been hiding in and "once I stepped back . . ." I experienced a ping of hope, a moment of personal triumph, a shred of dignity. Why? Because "I liked what I saw." Suddenly I had a visual boundary, a starting point, an opportunity to reenter life.

Today, if I could map my trek to wellness and draw you a visual of the path I've been on, it wouldn't fit inside the outline of my home state of Michigan. Nor would it fit inside the twenty-two hundred acres where the Tennessee cabin abides. Actually, it would require an atlas of the world. The trip (I did a lot of tripping) toward stability took me through jungles of emotions, pits of despair, ledges of fear, deserts of loneliness, wind shears of relationship, and white, churning waves of anger. Ah, but the vistas from mountaintops, the bounty in gardens, the beauty on beaches, the serenity inside forests, and the vibrancy of rainbows would cause the journey to have life-breathing purpose.

"Make your bed" was a divine doorway for me to reenter life. I know it sounds too simple and obvious to be a breakthrough; yet in that step-back moment, that's just what it was for my trapped heart. I should have known to get up and set things in order, but I was too overwhelmed and intent on someone else taking responsibility for my recovery. I didn't think I had what it would take to get well. I was neither brave nor competent. I would have to grow into those big-girl shoes.

How tender of the Lord to make the invitation toward change attainable. He knew it would take all I had to even make the bed, and he also knew I was desperate enough to finally risk trusting him for what I couldn't do. To look at myself through an achievement instead of from under blankets of weighty failure spurred me on; it offered me a new way of seeing.

I selected the theme "stained glass hearts" for this writing project for a number of reasons. First, I think even the phrase "stained glass" conjures up not only the usefulness of brokenness, but also its potential beauty. And even though the stained glass pieces are artistically designed, they still have been broken, sanded, and soldered. They didn't naturally fit the redemptive pattern without holy repairs. Also, stained glass art doesn't begin to show its beauty or its inspiration or release its story until light touches the dark. The light transforms an otherwise subtle picture into a brilliant, dimensional experience.

Isn't that how we are? Broken? Sharp edges? In need of repair? Longing to be, yet frightened of being, seen in the light? I know I'm all of the above and then some. And I deeply identify with the stained heart: tainted by my own spiteful nature, disruptive and addictive tendencies, with longings for my life story to be infused with purpose and meaning.

In the chapters ahead I have included elements that have spiritually nurtured my heart, and I hope they will yours as well. At the close of each chapter, you'll find a section called "The Art Gallery." It will include quotes, poetry, music, scriptures, artists, and more.

My suggestions of, say, art may send you on a quest to a library or the Internet, and the music may take you to iTunes. This will be an interactive adventure during which I think you will find the stories, songs, and pictures inspiring, comforting, heart-expanding, and revealing.

Sometimes simple is profound. And sometimes the answer for change in our lives is so close we can miss it . . . unless we gain God's perspective. Hopefully our art, music, and book exploration will give us some step-back time. And then we can begin to "enjoy the view."

Friend and author Ian Cron said to me, "Christianity is not something we do; it's something that gets done to us."

So true. I wish that thought could be etched into the stained glass windows of our souls. Our faith journey is about grace, and grace is such a scandal because it whispers that *it's not about our efforts but about God's provisional love.* That's so hard to embrace because in our humanity we are certain if we try harder, serve more, love better, we will somehow earn our wholeness and make points with God.

When God whispered, "Make your bed" to my fear-ravaged heart, he knew I needed to move out of my self-made hiding place, which had become a dungeon for my soul, and to step into the light of his grace.

Today at times I still wrestle with my tendency to think

that what I do qualifies me before God instead of what he's done and completed. In my mind I know the truth, but my emotions still are susceptible to the lies of the evil one as he bellows, "You haven't done enough!" "You aren't enough!" "Try harder!" I have a natural leaning toward legalism, strapping myself to works and buying the lies. I'm grateful the gift of God's love continues to liberate me and help me to *see* Christ in his grace-based holiness and to see others and myself with our delicately designed stained glass hearts, each with a redemptive story to tell . . . In the pages ahead are some of those stories.

How 'bout we get started?

Chapter 2

Achy-Breaky Hearts

Today I stood on a broken heart.

That felt odd.

And even though it was a mosaic set into the floor in a studio where I was recording sound bites for radio, it seemed personal. I mean, I was smack-dab in the middle of that tragic art. Actually, when I think about it, I've known people who have stood on my achy-breaky heart, and I think that's why it felt inappropriate to stand center stage on that delicate design.

When I finished my recording time and headed for home, the mosaic stayed on my mind. *Whose fractured heart have I stood on, adding to their pain?* I asked myself.

Ouch. Immediately names popped up in my head—and those were just the ones I knew. I found myself wanting to retreat from my own inquisition. Instead, I stood on the outer edge of responsibility and took furtive glances at my past behavior.

I don't know about you, but it took a lot of years before I realized my parents were, well, full-fledged, bona fide, pulse-bearing people. Oh, I knew they were capable of a range of emotions, but being a self-absorbed child, it never occurred to me that my thoughtless choices actually hurt them. I figured it was in their job description to make me happy and deflect (not correct) my rebellious behavior without reaction or complaint. Of course, they had other ideas.

It took me decades before I realized parents' goals aren't to make their children happy but healthy, humane, and civil, which in return causes those children to be better-adjusted, compassionate humans, which interestingly enough makes them happy people.

My parents had waited a long time for a little girl, so I was a welcome bundle. My brother was nine years older than I was, and he understandably was reluctant to toss confetti at my ruffled appearance because it greatly altered the relational dynamics and demands in our home. Often Don became my babysitter, a job he never volunteered for and which didn't help endear me to him. He wanted to play ball with his buddies and date girls, not babysit "brats." And brat I was, outspoken and selfish beyond healthy limits.

My mother had many rules, but she and my dad indulged me emotionally. May I just say that indulgence results in pouty, whiny, lazy children? I soon learned that when I applied those behaviors, I could sidestep rules and get what I wanted. In no time I became a skilled manipulator. Unfortunately, with that poor skill set I went from being a spoiled child to becoming a runaway teenager, to ending up a depressed young adult who didn't know how to fit into a reciprocal world of relationships full of expectations.

Unlearning ingrained habits isn't easy, especially those behaviors we unconsciously assimilate as children. It was never my parents' goal to raise a difficult child; their intentions were good, but their skills were lacking. Today I have great empathy for my parents because I am one, and I've lived long enough to see my own parenting deficiencies (and any I missed that my kids have willingly, yet lovingly, pointed out).

Our behavior as adults often reveals what we learned or didn't learn as children to survive the mosaic world we grew up in. Owning our self-serving ways can be intimidating because it feels so personal, as if it's about who we are rather than how we behave. Behavior is not ironclad proof of our desires but instead highlights skills we learned early on . . . unless at some point we consciously chose to hang on to our childishness, and now it has become synonymous with whom we have purposed to become.

Whew, that was a mouthful. I'm sure that's why, in the love chapter of Corinthians, we are entreated to "put away childish things" (1 Corinthians 13:11 KJV). There comes a time when we need to give up unproductive, immature, self-serving ways—which, again, is a process. It's not natural to deny ourselves.

So allow me to take a detour from the achy-breaky theme of this chapter to the curing of those heart fractures by sharing a little of my recovery. Let me say God works differently in each of our lives according to his greater plan and our greater good; yet his principles stay consistent throughout the ages.

Recovering from an overdose of self is exhausting. It takes divine grit, courage, and assistance. Without a doubt we need God's help, the One who drew up the original blueprint for our best selves. And we need the help of others on the journey, those who have and are working on their own stuff. We weren't meant to recover alone.

When looking for assistance, don't assume that because people have accumulated years, they have necessarily become refined in character. Instead, whatever their age, take note of the fruit in their lives. How do they live love? Joy? Peace? Have they endured and grown through hardship? Are they rattled easily, or is peace engrained in their responses?

While we aren't looking for perfection, we are looking for measurable maturity, a steadiness that comes with relinquishment and trust. When you find a humble heart, which is a key result of growth, sidle up to that person and take notes. Careful observation can expedite your own healing, as often we learn by example.

As I thought back through some of the more difficult years of my life, I pulled out three mosaic pieces that helped position me for change and helped me form a new perspective. These are steps I had to take for myself, with God's help. No one could do these for me.

1. Own childish behavior.
2. Move toward change.
3. Think differently.

If we don't agree with what's true about ourselves, we don't change. It's that simple and that hard. Truth, while liberating, initially can be scary and feel disassembling. Don't let that throw you. Actually, those shaky feelings are good signs that you are on the right path. Once we are willing to face what's true about ourselves, we can begin the demanding work that change requires. (You'll need a hard hat, overalls, tools, and no less than a trough full of sweat, if you want change. It's not for satisfied sissies.)

My hubby, Les, grew up in a home of industrious people. Everybody worked. Everybody pitched in. Even though his dad was cruel in most ways, he did teach his children a strong work ethic, which, generally speaking, has served them well.

I, on the other hand, spent my childhood slipping out of tasks and dreading work. So when Les and I married, he did far more tasks around the house than he should have, filling in for his self-indulgent wife. Change didn't become measurable in me until I finally pulled myself out of bed before noon and tackled daily chores.

I, too, grew up around industrious people, especially my mom, who had a tendency to do everything for all of us. That approach isn't healthy. Not for the person who is constantly overextending herself (and who often comes to resent it), or for the ones who aren't learning how to share in the workload. Serving others might be your love language, but indulging underdeveloped individuals around you is no gift to anyone. Check the quality of fruit you are producing in others by your efforts. Is what you are doing adding character substance to their lives?

Quite honestly, in the beginning of my change, my depression was so thick and my self-indulgence button so stuck, all I could do was ready myself for a day. One chore I began doing regularly, as I've mentioned, was making my bed. Initially that was no easy task.

I had to push through the foreboding cloud in my head and learn that discipline is about constancy. Developing discipline is mentally sweaty work because it begins in our entrenched attitudes—so bring a shovel. In time and with herculean effort, I also picked up things, washed dishes, did laundry, and eventually fixed meals (frozen fare . . . it was a start).

Now I've grown so fastidious about my home that I require chats with myself to "lighten up." I even give myself permission to sometimes not make my bed, as a reminder that a few rumpled blankets don't indict my character. My tendency is to flip and then flop from one extreme to another.

I used to think of myself as worthless one moment and exceptional the next. Exceptional was always fleeting and was quickly followed by the rapid tumble back down into the pit of worthlessness. It took a lot of work to find a "normal" on my radar.

I find balance to be a delicate position to attain, one that is easily jarred and tipped. When taken to the extreme, even happy is a sure ticket to sad. If I allow myself to get too high on happy, to the point of giddiness, I find my scale is skewed, and I pay the price of an emotional low.

My friend Anna was reminded of balance when in her attempt to do things well and correctly she brushed her teeth daily with great vigor, only to be told by her dentist that she was going to "brush herself into a root canal." Even a good habit, when overdone, can become wearing.

Now that he's retired, Les still helps with tasks around the house, but we have a much healthier balance of give-and-take. He no longer feels obligated to overdo, and I no longer have unfair expectations. Usually.

Is there something in your life that you should be doing but that you've assigned to someone else? While you may have been successful in getting rid of a responsibility, it has been my experience that you have given away a chunk of your self-esteem. Begin doing your own tasks; it's a starting place for developing a stronger work ethic and a healthier regard for yourself. And might I mention it is God's way that we all pull our own weight and tend to our assignments?

Don't be surprised if the person who's been filling in for you is initially reluctant to give up his or her add-on tasks. Many times people have their own issues, and feeling an unhealthy obligation is one of them. Also their need for credit can be askew. Thank them for their willingness, but hold on to your resolve to do what is yours to accomplish. Remember, it isn't wrong to accept help, but we must weigh carefully the price paid by all when we don't assume responsibility for our part.

A number of years ago a friend took me aback when she casually mentioned what a hard worker I was. "I am?" I replied, surprised someone viewed me in that manner. She went on to tell me all the ways she had observed how diligently I had applied myself to what needed to be done. It was heart-healthy for me to hear from someone who had been taking notes on me. I had been so busy trying to do the right thing that at times I missed the joy of change and growth. Don't forget to give yourself an occasional pat on the back and regular hallelujahs to the One who empowers us to change. Voicing acknowledgment of God's ongoing deliverance in our lives reminds us of his loving-kindness on our behalf, which is especially important to those of us who have questioned his intentions and love toward us. And it puts things into a holy perspective.

During the process of realizing I could command my lazy muscles to get up and move, I found my thought-life about work was vitally important. Scripture has much to say about diligence, and I began to search the Bible for "work counsel."

So instead of dreading a chore, I could look forward to the good feelings that came with completing my tasks. Even when I didn't feel good, I knew I had done what I should, which is a building block for mental health. And I saw that work could be a physical way of expressing love and servanthood toward God and others. Disciplined choices became my contribution to restoring order to the world, or at least my world. And what fanned that flame of discipline were grateful thoughts, experiencing the joy in a hard day's work, and verses that helped to form new rhythms in my behavior, such as "Serve the LORD with gladness" (Psalm 100:2).

Okay, now about achy hearts . . .

My need to circle back to my parents to confess my insensitive and selfish behavior and to ask for their forgiveness for my deliberate rebellion was important to me. This allowed us to establish a healthier connection, it made room for changed behavior, and it affirmed my heart's progress.

Please reread that last sentence. Don't underestimate or sidestep this vital part of reconciliation and redemption. For those of you whose loved ones have passed away, may I say it's never too late to walk through confession and forgiveness in prayer?

But the proof of my truly being different was in changed behavior; so I found in the early days of my recovery I needed to keep my talk about how I was going to change at a minimum and my actions at a maximum. I found too much prechange chatter depleted my resolve, proving the old adage "Actions speak louder than words."

My young-adult immaturity touched a number of people, but probably none more than my husband. We were teenagers when we married, and I was demanding and depressed. Not an easy blend to live with, especially when you add in a critical and sarcastic spirit.

Today I realize that sarcasm is anger gone underground that's reemerged in a clown's suit. And while a sarcastic comment can be funny, mostly it's not. No matter how many times we say, "I was only kidding," sarcasm chisels away at the soul, inflicting wounds and creating distance.

Les, too, battles with being sarcastic; so we both have to guard our hearts and minds from this tendency and at times from each other. It's not easy establishing new boundaries in a marriage. We've had to make some grace-space for the times we fall back into old behaviors because we know we'll need to extend grace to each other as long as we are in these earth suits. Likewise we have to guard smudging the grace extended to us with our retaliatory tendencies. Getting even is never even; it's an unending teeter-totter ride because while one person is temporarily elevated by sarcasm, the other one is jolted and down for the count.

After forty-eight years of marriage, Les and I still are learning how to speak the truth in love, how to allow love to cover offenses, and how not to use humor as a covert operation to hurt each other. We are learning how to come alongside each other's mosaic heart instead of standing smack-dab in the middle of it and, yes, at times jumping up and down on it like a trampoline. We're learning to respect each other's delicate design.

When you think about it, love is a holy art, not a holy war. I don't want to live on the rim of responsibility; I want to move into the center of God's plan that I "grow up in all aspects"—a lifelong process. Just because some of us have grown old, we haven't necessarily grown up. And even if "we've come a long way, baby," there's still more we can learn, change, and do.

If you're younger, don't underestimate the power of your influence and of a life well lived.

May we learn not to add to each other's pain and not to

deliberately take potshots at each other's fractures. There's enough hardship in this world. Instead, with God's help, may we walk softly on the landscape of each other's hearts, understanding the terrain is fragile.

My favorite part of the mosaic set in the floor at the studio was that every piece of the broken heart was there. Humpty Dumpty was another deal. His parts were strewn to the point that even a posse couldn't gather them up. Unlike poor Humpty, we have a Creator who knows where the scattered pieces of our achy-breaky hearts landed and how to fit them back together again. Not one splinter escapes his redemptive work. Our restoration will be an ongoing integration until the day we step into Christ's presence, when all will finally be set into place.

The Art Gallery

Mosaics: If you were to take a trip to visit mosaics, you could literally circle the globe. From Jordan to Barcelona, from Cairo to London, from Washington, DC, to Mexico City, from Jerusalem to the New York subways, you'd be dizzy with wonder at the amazing beauty and intricacies of this art. (Yes, hundreds of mosaics reside in the underbelly of the New York transit. Don't miss the hats! Delightfully innovative.)

Mosaics are made from broken bits of colored stone, glass, terra-cotta, shells, and so on. Why, you can even use cut-up credit cards as fodder to design a mosaic something-or-other (lampshade, picture frame, earrings). The magic of a mosaic is that up close you see the colorful details, but when you back away, you see the bigger view of how brokenness comes together to form astonishing art . . . like gaining perspective on a life that Christ redeems.

Go online to Google and explore the world of mosaics. You'll find them in churches, cathedrals, palaces, spas, and your girlfriend's powder room (which will not be on Google). Once you start looking, you'll be surprised how prevalent they are in museums, furniture details, swimming pools, aquariums, and outdoor patio paraphernalia.

Google the words "ancient mosaics" and be fascinated. Just think how many broken things we've thrown away that could have been incorporated into usable art. Why, in broken glasses alone I could have paved the L.A. freeways. Hmm. That might be ticklish on tires . . . never mind.

Visit Wikipedia under "Byzantine Art" for a brief education and to see mosaic pictures from around the world.

Church: Investigate the National Cathedral, officially known as the Cathedral Church of Saint Peter and Saint Paul, in Washington, DC. It has breathtaking architecture, including mosaics throughout. It also holds the remains of many notables, including Helen Keller and Ann Sullivan . . . who left us a "mosaic" with their life stories. It is by far my favorite place to visit in DC.

Visiting the church will make you feel as if you took a trip to Europe. And while you're at it, take note of the beautiful work by Frederick Hart, called *The Creation Sculpture*, over the entry. I was so taken by the motion, beauty, and energy Hart achieved that I have a professional photograph of that work hanging in my home. Hart was a relatively unknown artist until he won the opportunity to do this assignment. The time Hart spent at the cathedral changed his life and started him on a path of faith.

YouTube: Mosaic Art Works-Mosaic Art School, Ravenna, Italy, will take you on a tour of a mosaic art school. You never know; you may want to capture your mother-in-law's image in stone for posterity. You might. Someday. Maybe.

Music: "Broken Hallelujah," Mandisa

Chapter 3

Enlarge Our Hearts, Oh, Lord

Speaking of perspective—we were, weren't we?—a few years ago my eldest son, Marty, came into my office and sat down, wearing a satisfied grin. He had just come from the optometrist, and he was sporting new glasses. A change in Marty's prescription was long overdue; he was pleased to once again have a crystal-clear view of the world.

I was giving my approval of the way they looked on him when I noticed a smudge on his lenses. I had just purchased tear-off paper tissues for my glasses, and they were on my desk.

"Hand me your glasses," I ordered, as I reached for the packet of tissues.

Marty complied, and I scrubbed the smudge into oblivion. This pleased me. Then, to make sure both lenses were sparkling, I swirled the paper over the other one as well. Marty then pulled on his glasses and slowly looked around the room. Too slowly. I watched as an odd look followed by dismay slipped across his face.

"What's wrong?" I asked, thinking him unappreciative of my effort.

"You scratched them," he said softly.

"No, I didn't. Let me see."

Sure enough, I had ground scratches deep into his spanking new lenses. Had I read the "read this first" booklet that came with his glasses, I would have seen that they required a special soft cloth. My heart sank . . . as did his. Marty then spent the next year peering at life through mother-inflicted scribbles. The joy of seeing life from a clear perspective lasted less than thirty minutes.

Marty, my firstborn, tends to be a perfectionist but only in certain areas . . . for example, his eyeglasses. But at least outwardly he handled my blunder well. Marty is skilled electronically and mechanically, so seeing clearly matters. He is much like his dad in that way—and also in displaying courage.

This past fall Marty hadn't been feeling well. Each day he seemed a little worse than the day before. He was living in Michigan while his dad and I were in Tennessee.

Early one morning, much to my surprise, I woke up as though someone had given me a good shake. I sat up in bed with a sudden realization that Marty's ailment was threatening his life. I prayed the word *mercy* over and over again. "Oh, Lord, please have mercy on our son."

After a while Les woke up, perhaps because I was hovering an inch over his face, watching to see when his eyes would open. When they did, I blurted out, "Marty is in danger and needs to go to the emergency room!"

Les was trying to weigh the validity of my urgency through

his sleep-clouded mind when a friend of ours from Michigan called. Les asked Carl if he would run Marty over to the emergency clinic and let the doctors take a look at him.

Upon Marty's arrival and after taking his vital signs, the clinic personnel called for an ambulance to rush him to the hospital. The doctors at the hospital immediately put Marty into a medical coma and placed him on life support. Our son had H1N1, pneumonia, and a severe sinus infection, and he wasn't expected to live.

Marty spent the next twenty-one days on a ventilator and miraculously survived. His life today is physically difficult. His joints are full of arthritis, and the medical community can do little to alleviate the distress in his body caused by the virus, his medicines, and his coma.

During our hospital vigil, Les and I took shifts as we waited to see what God had planned. Many times our hearts were so full of pain it was difficult to breathe deeply. It's still hard to talk about that time because it throws me back into scary feelings of helplessness. Until the doctor took Marty off the ventilator, we didn't know if he would survive; so for twenty-one days we held our breath, waiting to see if he could maintain his.

As I peer back through the dark clouds of that uncertain journey, a few thoughts emerge as life-sustaining for our family. And because this is a book about light and redemption, I thought it made sense to spotlight those redeeming moments in the valley of the shadow of death.

I've been aware for years of how prayer comforts the human

heart. Yet I was taken aback during this death-valley walk by the undergirding prayers that sustained us. They were palpable. I literally could feel the prayers of God's people holding me steady as I moved around Marty's bedside, through the hospital's halls, and when I would lay my head down to rest. The prayers quieted my mind and heart so I could sleep. When a turbulent current of despair would threaten to swell, the prayers acted as a barrier to direct the rising panic away from me.

Many people wrote daily on my Facebook page to let me know that they continued to pray for Marty. The visual encouragement of those posts was like personal visits. Because Marty was contagious and was in a unit full of others with communicable diseases, we insisted our friends and family stay away. We could have felt all alone in this heartache if it weren't for texts, Tweets, e-mails, Facebook postings, and cell calls.

Mary Graham, friend and president of Women of Faith, sent text messages to me several times each day. Many times she simply said, "I love you."

I had forgotten how powerful those words are when you're battling your way through fear and pain. Scripture reminds us that "perfect love casts out fear, because fear involves punishment" (1 John 4:18). Mary's love notes often gave me the impetus to take the next step. Love instills courage.

Even though folks couldn't safely come to the hospital, people found creative ways to show their love and support. One group of dear friends sent us coupons to a favorite eating place in our hometown. Then, whenever our need would arise for food on the run, we could pop in as we drove through town to pick up sustenance. It was a godsend.

Trust me, it takes focus for me to produce edible offerings, and while my mind and emotions were stretched so thin, I wasn't in any condition to handle hot pans and sharp knives. Besides, if I wasn't at the hospital, I was facedown in bed, trying to rest up for the next shift.

My friend Jan Silvious was a steady phone voice in the gale winds of our story. I knew whenever I needed to talk, she would listen; and when I needed input, she gently would advise. A trusted friend who is tracking with you in her availability and her prayers is a stabilizing force.

One day I arrived at the hospital, walked past the coffee shop, the gift store, down the now-familiar halls to a bank of elevators and pushed the "up" button. I realized we had developed a hospital rhythm, knowing every turn and twist without thinking. As the doors drew open, I leaned forward to step in and then saw something that made me jump back in confusion. There stood my friends Tami and her husband, Dale, who lived in another state.

My muddled brain was having trouble figuring out how they could be in this elevator. As we hugged, I realized how wonderful it was to have friends share our pain face-to-face. It turned out they were on a business trip that took them to the same city as the hospital, and they didn't want to leave without expressing their concern and love.

Before we arrived Tami and Dale had scrubbed up, suited

up, gone into Marty's room, stood at the foot of his bed, and prayed for him. Not knowing they would bump into Les and me as they left, they placed a love note next to Marty's bedside, which I would read and reread in the days ahead.

Later when I stepped into Marty's room, I felt the strength of their prayers still lingering. I didn't realize how tenderly my heart would be touched, knowing others had added their life-giving, spoken prayers into this machine-congested, beeping, buzzing, sterile environment. Their hearts, enlarged with love, had touched mine.

We don't always know what we need in a crisis until someone provides it. Then, and sometimes not until later, we realize how significant each contribution was to our sanity and to fan fresh hope into our spirits.

There's no doubt about it: prayers and people matter.

The next thing that was a strong reminder during this chapter of our lives was "change can be good." I'm all for change, actually—if I'm the one implementing it. Otherwise, I can find it threatening, which is what happened the day I arrived at the hospital and was told they were moving Marty from one intensive care unit to another in the same hospital.

"Why?" was my insistent question that wasn't being answered in a way that satisfied my anxious heart. I could hear my voice intensifying; then a thought rolled into my mind: *What if this change is for good?*

The thought seemed unreasonable because I couldn't make sense of why the medical staff would change his care by what seemed to me to be a disruptive move. But the thought *What if this change is for good?* planted itself in my mind and wouldn't be shaken loose.

I confess that I've been wrong many times. My conclusions haven't always aligned with outcomes. So when this reminder, *What if this change is for good?*, tattooed itself in my head, I didn't want to ignore it in case I blindly stood in the way of a breakthrough for our son. And yet . . . I didn't want to stand back and allow the hospital staff to make a choice that further threatened Marty's life either.

A doctor assured me repeatedly there was no danger in the physical move; yet before they could get Marty into the new bed, he went into crisis. A flurry of running nurses surrounded him and worked to stabilize him. I was frozen outside his room, listening to their efforts when a male nurse joined them. Within a minute or two, he had discovered and corrected the problem, and all the life-support machines settled back into their rhythm. It would take longer for my erratic heartbeats to do the same.

I wasn't informed until after the move that all Marty's doctors would be different because he had changed floors. This set me off into an emotional tizzy. I felt that was a risky idea. The original doctors were familiar with his case while the new doctors would have to learn it. This seemed like lost time to me, which Marty couldn't afford. But the drumbeat of *What if this change is for good?* remained, and I tried, in a knee-shaking way, to trust that the thought was from the Lord.

The new team of doctors arrived, headed up by a woman who was assertive and verbally direct. Obviously she was in command. Then she spotted my husband and me seated on a bench near the door to Marty's room. She pointed at us and demanded, "Who are they?" I announced we were Marty's parents, to which she commanded, "You may sit there, but you may not talk."

I didn't say a word, but I could feel my blood pressure rising. I scrutinized the doctor's every move. I watched as she picked up a list of Marty's meds, scanned down them, and then asked for a phone. One of her assistants handed it to her, and she called the in-house pharmacy, where she asked—no, demanded—that one of the meds be changed immediately. After what sounded like a verbal scuffle, the matter was settled, and the change was made. That call turned out to be a breakthrough, as I would find out the following morning.

Then the doctor asked, "How long has this man been on the ventilator?" When she heard it had been twenty days, she said, "What? Twenty days? Why, he'll be loopy. We have to get him off of it."

When those words touched my ears, my first thought was, *This change could be good.* No one had been talking about removing his ventilator until she entered the scene.

By morning Marty's lingering sinus infection was gone because of the medicine change made the night before. One of the doctors met me when I arrived and had me go into a side room while they removed Marty's ventilator. I couldn't believe it was happening. My heart was ricocheting with both excitement and fear. Finally I was told I could go in to see him.

For the first time since admittance, our son was sitting up and breathing on his own. I rushed to his side and placed my hands on his arm. To my surprise, Marty jerked his arm away from me and whispered through his raw throat, "Don't touch me!"

I was shocked. I thought all my son's mother issues must have come up in his coma. I backed away to comply. Then he turned and weakly motioned to the nurse to come near, and he whispered, "Am I still contagious?"

"Oh, no, you haven't been contagious for some time," she assured him.

Marty turned back in my direction and motioned me toward him. I leaned forward so I could hear his raspy voice. He said, "Kiss me."

"Kiss you?" I asked, to make sure I understood what he was asking, and he nodded his head. I quickly complied. (Later my friend Marilyn Meberg reminded me that our greatest human need is connection. Marty's request made perfect sense.)

Need I tell you how relieved I was to know that Marty's initial reaction was his desire to protect me and not to reject me? I gave birth to Marty when I was twenty years old. I was ill prepared for motherhood or real life. Within two years of his birth, I became phobic, and Marty grew up in the unstable atmosphere of my frayed emotions.

So when he said, "Don't touch me," I knew he had reasons

to have mother issues. Early on, when he was impressionable, I had smudged the lenses of his life perspective with my fears, and it would take time for him to see beyond the ground-in scratches of my brokenness and to get new lenses of his own.

I'm grateful that love not only instills courage, but it also covers a multitude of sins, including mother-inflicted scribbles.

Prayer matters. People matter. Change can be good. And ultimately, love rules.

The Art Gallery

Museum: *Detroit Institute of Art, Mother and Child*, painted in 1881 by Enoch Wood Perry. A tender scene set in the contrast of sunlight and shadows.

My daughter-in-law, Danya, and our shared friend Leslie visited the Detroit Institute of Art recently and came back very excited. One of the pieces that had captured their imaginations was of a nun who stepped into a hospital room only to discover her long-lost love, Gabriel, dying in a bed. She has brought flowers, not knowing to whom they would be given, but upon seeing her old love, she drops the vase, and flowers lay scattered at her feet.

Surrounding this scene in an open room are nurses and a patient, all captivated by the story unfolding in front of them. The painting is based on the poem "Evangeline" by Henry Wadsworth Longfellow and was created from 1887 to 1889 by Samuel Richards.

Poem: "Evangeline." This poem is involved and lengthy, so I suggest you assemble a cup of tea, a notebook, and perhaps a poem-savvy friend before you wade in. While it's not easy to follow, it contains beautiful imagery. "Evangeline" is about love, loss, and death.

Prayer: Oh, God who is near to the brokenhearted, please make yourself known, for our pain threatens to blind us to your nearness, and our fears deafen us with their scary recitals that are ever clanging in our ears.

God-Man, who conquered death, remove our grave clothes of panic and pessimism. Wrap us in the life-bearing mantle of praise. Your intentions are holy and glorious, while we become so easily shrouded in the shadows of self-serving matters. Rescue us from small speculations. Enlarge our hearts.

You alone, Lord, can attend to our desperation. Silence us with your peace. Comfort us with your tenderness. Mend us with your love. Amen.

Music: "He Is with You," Mandisa; "Held," Natalie Grant; "Goodbye for Now," Kathy Troccoli

---

Chapter 4

Reflections on Our Heart Condition

Recently in a packing-up-to-move effort, I unearthed an old eyeglass case containing a once-stylish pair of spectacles. Actually, when I slipped them on, I was the spectacle. It wasn't just that they were no longer chic with their overdone, glitzy frames, but the prescription was so outdated I could hardly see myself in the mirror. My outline was wobbly, my features distorted, and because I had to strain to see through the lenses, they were giving me an instant headache. They weren't scratched like my son's, but they might as well have been because my eyes had changed so much my view through them was a blur.

When I thought about my "viewing" problem with those flashy glasses, I was reminded of the struggle I've had most of my life in seeing myself kindly. Long before I wore glasses, my mirror told distorted stories like the mirrors at the circus that allow us to appear twelve feet tall one moment and a squatty mouse the next, or they reflect a misshapen face as if it had been jammed into a soda bottle, then uncorked for others to laugh at. We chuckle at our circus images, knowing that what we see isn't accurate, but the reflections in our own mirrors, now, that can be a more sobering story.

"Mirror, mirror, on the wall . . ." the line from a childhood story highlights vanity, jealousy, and revenge. The mirror has had countless stories, poems, and plays penned about its often troubling viewpoint. And yet we have mirrors hanging throughout our homes, restaurants, businesses, and churches. We even carry portable ones tucked inside our pockets and purses. Are we vain beyond measure? Or do you think we're saying, "See me; I matter"? Or is it as silly—and profound—as our losing track of ourselves in this congested world, and we're checking to see if we've disappeared into the melee of life?

Mirrors do cause rooms to look larger and light to bounce around spaces, brightening the corners where we live. In our current home, we have built-in mirrored medicine cabinets over the sink, which were meant to be functional. But all I can see in them is the top of my spiky hair. When I turn around, the closet doors are full-length mirrors, startling me with far more information than I care to know. I keep expecting a siren to go off and a voice to insist, "Oversharing, oversharing!"

On a ledge above my sink I've placed a pack of personalized Scripture cards that I now stare at while I tidy up, instead of growling at the morning mirror. This has worked out well.

In the book of James we are told, "Be ye doers of the word, and not hearers only, deceiving your own selves. For if any be a hearer of the word, and not a doer, he is like unto a man beholding his natural face in a glass: For he beholdeth himself, and goeth his way, and straightway forgetteth what manner of man he was" (James 1:22–24 KJV).

Well, ain't that the truth? I peek in a mirror to check out my new haircut, and by the time I walk home a block and a half away, I've forgotten how it looks. I stand in front of a looking glass and spend time trying to memorize it, only to find myself headed back down the hall throughout the day to glance once again at my hairdo. Maybe hoping it will improve.

I've decided mirrors and eyeglasses should all be made from the hues in stained glass windows. Oh, I know we couldn't see well, but life and our reflections would be radiantly colorful, gardens would always be in bloom, people would be vibrant and bright, and even our jobs would sparkle. And think how all those colors would help elevate our moods.

But I guess such perfection sounds more like heaven than earth. So, really, what's our best hope here and now for seeing ourselves in a better light, viewing others from a positive perspective, and looking up to God with a clearer understanding of his heart, which is full for us?

Years ago I was at a conference during which a singer was performing the beautiful yet simple song that many of us were introduced to as children at Sunday school, "Jesus Loves Me." The slow, almost bluesy, rendition was stunning, causing a hush to come over the auditorium of thousands of women. Suddenly in the middle of the song, a young woman in the balcony had a swelling outburst of emotions. First it was faint but grew quickly to heaving sobs as she repeatedly cried out, "He loves me, he loves me!"

Undoubtedly an unforgettable moment for that young woman, it stirred those of us who were in the auditorium with her. Her discovery was palpable: Jesus loved her decidedly, tenderly, intimately.

In those holy moments Christ's love registered deep within her. I think when we "get" God's love, really get it, so that we internalize it, our view of life changes. Circumstances don't necessarily change; yet suddenly, as if we just donned much-needed glasses, for the first time we see that hardships have purpose, we see why the moments of our days matter, we see ourselves on a directed path, and we see that people's impact on us is both neutralized *and* amplified for good.

How do we go about experiencing such a breakthrough moment? Hire someone to sing until we feel God's love? Faith is much more than feelings; yet feelings are certainly an integral part of our identities and therefore important to the One who designed us. But there is also a knowing that God's Spirit ignites within us that seems to solidify our confidence in his love. I believe God is ever present in his longing for our attention and affection. His love is ever wooing because of his constancy. And sometimes, rather than as a sudden breakthrough, our knowing comes as a gradual awakening, like a rose unfolding into full bloom. We grow into an understanding of how deeply he cares for us.

I remember the morning at a country church when I asked

Christ to redeem my life. At that juncture I was confused, sad, afraid, angry, and desperate. The pastor prayed with me, and when I walked out the door of that tiny chapel, I had a breakthrough moment.

The sky had never seemed so clear, the sun had never shone so bright, and the grass was a vivid green carpet beneath my feet, bidding me to step into life. I didn't say anything to anyone about what I was experiencing lest it disappear or someone smudge my experience with his doubt.

I arrived at my parents' house, and I knew something significant had happened to me on the inside when I looked out their picture window. They lived on a lake that I always had felt was threatening, but this day when I looked out, the water shimmered with beauty. I couldn't get out the front door fast enough and ran down to the dock to stand near the lake's mirrored beauty. I just knew I had been given a new way of seeing life and that the colorful displays in nature would last forever.

Did all that colorful display last? Nope. The hope would rise up again but not the intense colors or the Pollyanna optimism. Life has a way of clouding over and raining on our parades. Have you noticed?

When I had my first emotionally unsettling day after my chapel experience, my heart sank with disappointment. I guess I thought God had not only redeemed me from my lost condition and given me new lenses through which to view life but also had mended my broken heart and reknitted my frayed emotions in one fell swoop. I didn't realize there is the instantaneous salvation of our hearts and then there is the ongoing daily path of redemption, as we learn to walk and talk with Christ. I wanted one dip in the pool and, voilà, perfection and ease. Instead I found that life still was hard, people were difficult, and I still was bumbling about, tripping over my misconceptions and inadequacies.

I'm grateful that through Bible study and the people whom Christ brought across my path to teach me by their examples, I learned how to see with a healthy optimism. God's people held up the mirror of what they had learned, and I found the color in life even on stormy days.

When I was struggling with thundering emotions, my friend Rose would find Scripture passages that she would have me read aloud to her. They were verses that mirrored truth about my behavior and supplied hope for change. Rose knew God's Word had far more influence over me than if she had offered her opinions. Besides, it's much harder to debate God, and my friend was tired of ducking the lightning strikes of my angry rebuttals. We both knew I could outtalk her, but under the scrutiny of God's counsel, I was silenced.

At times, trusting God in the minutia of life is as difficult as trusting him for a walking-on-water miracle. For me, especially in the beginning steps of faith, I held on tight fisted to unhealthy behaviors, thinking that because they were familiar, they were both right and safe.

I found that when you shift beliefs, the dismantling of your thoughts is like changing a roof on a house, in that suddenly your interior feels exposed to the elements. When you're not used to fresh breezes and sunlight, they can feel intimidating and blinding rather than restorative. It takes time and hard work to secure new beams, not to mention the repetitive retiling process that needs to take place.

Speaking of retiling, I'm told our brain paves pathways when we have a thought and that thought, when received as truth, becomes a belief and a behavior. The more we think that thought, the more we nail down the information it transmits until the behavior settles in as a habit.

For instance, I believed outside environments and people created my feelings of panic and flooded me with frightening physical symptoms. Actually it was my belief that I wasn't safe that incited and fired up my emotions. When I felt scared or angry, I attached danger to my feelings, creating a firestorm of terror. Adrenaline would race through my body, setting off a myriad of symptoms: tremors, sweats, air hunger, racing thoughts.

I finally came to the realization that I was stirring up my own anxiety by believing the lies that I was going to die or lose my mind. When I admitted to myself that I had suffered through hundreds of anxiety attacks and yet I was still alive and sound of mind, the entrenched, scary thoughts began to lose their power over me.

I memorized Scripture that I would quote to redirect my thoughts toward God's care of me. I selected portions that mirrored his love and constancy. "God is our refuge and strength, an ever-present help in trouble" (Psalm 46:1 NIV). "He will never leave you nor forsake you" (Deuteronomy 31:6 NIV). "You are my hiding place" (Psalm 32:7 NIV).

I had a hard time believing that God loved me and that I could trust him to protect me. I thought that if he loved me, he would have rescued me from the panic that pursued and imprisoned me. I didn't understand that God had made me with a will stronger than any emotion I could experience and that I could begin to get well by choosing different thoughts and different actions. We come equipped, by God's design, with our own rip cord and backup parachute. And he makes every jump with us. Who knew? Not me—not for a long time. I had been in emotional free fall.

I grew stronger inwardly every time I chose to believe God instead of my fierce fears. In time, by determined neglect, my fears reduced in intensity, and my faith flourished. When I gave up coddling fear, the panic subsided, and in time the symptoms faded. No one who suffers with panic believes we're coddling fear because we abhor it, but in truth we pump up fear's importance and cradle it to us when we believe that we have no choice in its dominance over us. Feelings are not facts. Feelings can come packaged in lies. Big. Fat. Ones. And we have to refuse to buy into their emotionally disassembling propaganda.

Exercising our wills in a new direction is more exhausting than a new workout program. Most of us don't leap from the bed and sprint out the door singing the "Hallelujah Chorus" as we head for the gym. Instead, we drag ourselves from between the sheets, force ourselves into our workout clothes, mentally push ourselves onto the stationary bike, and will our feet to move. We can expect the same kind of all-out effort when shaping up our minds and gaining control of our runaway emotions.

I found in my recovery days that I was susceptible to moods and addictions. I learned it was best for me to avoid certain input: sad movies, scary books, some types of music, news reports, and harsh people because they kept me emotionally off-kilter.

Also I worked on breaking my addictions to cigarettes (two packs per day), coffee (ten pots per day), and tranquilizers (four per day). The combination of being strung out on caffeine, nicotine, and meds (I am all for necessary drugs) caused physical chaos, which stirred up my hypochondriac tendencies.

Once I corralled my emotions by acts of my will, the quality of my life improved. When I purposed to read uplifting books and spend time with nurturing people, I noticed a shift inside me. Not only did I feel better about myself, but I also wanted to be better. I worked on improving my nutrition and my erratic sleep habits. I gradually gave up smoking, caffeine, and then weaned myself off tranquilizers.

After I gave up cigarettes and ate healthier meals, I gained weight, my hair thickened, and my eyes once again had a sparkle. My weight had plunged along with my self-esteem, causing me to avoid photographs and mirrors, but eventually that changed because when we do what we can to take care of ourselves, it shows. And it wasn't just because my physical health was being affected by better choices that I liked my reflection, but my insides were changing, and I felt more like a contributing adult in the world instead of a whiny spectacle.

Remember, life change is a process that requires time, hard work, and merciful inner messages. And for me, supportive people were imperative to reflect a healthy kind of normal since at best my norm was extreme. Friends and God's Word continue to help me exchange my old eyeglasses for the new lenses of a higher perspective that allows me to see God more clearly, myself more gently, and others more lovingly.

The Art Gallery

Artist: *Norman Rockwell*. I grew up adoring the artwork of Norman Rockwell. His paintbrush storytelling art was always homespun and often patriotic, featuring Boy Scouts, picnics, parades, and soldiers. You may remember Rockwell's work was featured on the cover of the *Saturday Evening Post*. Rockwell considered the *Post* the "greatest show window in America" for an illustrator; millions viewed his work through that format.

One of my favorite Rockwell paintings was of a young girl in front of a mirror who appears perplexed by her reflection: *Girl at Mirror*. You must Google it, even if you remember it, to refresh your memory of all the details.

Book: I encourage you to purchase *Windows of the Soul* by Ken Gire because: (a) the book is brilliant (my copy looks like hieroglyphics I have so many notations in it); and (b) it includes a list of searching questions about *Girl at Mirror* to help us see it more fully and make some applications to our lives.

Chapter 5

Enough to Make a Stained Glass Heart Sing

One of the ways God has lifted my perspective is through creation's music. Turning my eyeglasses to the heavens and my ear to the earth, I thrill at the melodies and harmonies I find there. For instance, I never tire of the sparrow's song. The perfect-pitch warble of this little bit of a bird delights me with the purity of its passion. Being a plain bird myself, I love that the sparrow doesn't have the snazzy flair of a redbird or the intimidating stature of the blue jay, but instead is a diminutive warbler in a housedress. (For years observers believed that only the male sparrows sang, but now scientists are changing their minds and credit us girls with a string of our own top ten tunes—thank you very much.)

Recently my friend Lauren and I were sharing tea in my kitchen as we celebrated her birthday. We heard the most glorious sound, and I said, "Listen, Lauren, a quartet is singing happy birthday to you." We made our way toward the joyful sounds and drew open the top half of my Dutch door. Sure enough, four sparrows had landed on the reach-out-and-touch rooftop next door, and they were crooning their little hearts out. We applauded.

The song sparrow sings up to ten different songs while the house sparrow only has a few notes that he repeats over and over, as if he hasn't heard them before. (I know people who do that with jokes.) It doesn't matter the season. From summer's blazing sun to winter's bitter chill, the sparrows' songs are heartfelt. Although their music, like ours, is more likely to be heard in its operatic fullness when the temperatures are warm and the sun is dappling the tree limbs with a flecked, stained glass beauty. Not all, but many sparrows wing south and west for the winter and then return in the spring with a chipper new song full of distant dew. In Tennessee the sparrows bear the winter with us, offering their musical repertoire full of hope to cheer us on through frosty days and windy nights.

> I once had a sparrow alight upon my shoulder for a moment, while I was hoeing in a village garden, and I felt that I was more distinguished by that circumstance than I should have been by any epaulet I could have worn.
>
> —HENRY DAVID THOREAU

What is there about a song that soothes, delights, inspires, and entertains us so? Is it that the words, instruments, and blended sound add such emotional color to our life perspective? How many times has a song helped you to access untouched feelings? When was the last time a song made you cry from the sheer beauty of its sound? "All I Ask of You" by Andrew Lloyd

Webber is one that leaves my tissues moist as I catch the tender content of my joy tipped by the song's elegance.

I think musical pieces are like stained glass windows in that a song contains many elements of color—from the words to the arrangement to the voice of instruments and vocals. When placed together, they form a story—a window into another's heart and likewise into our own hearts.

For the past few years, Sandi Patty has been a weekly road companion at the Women of Faith conferences. This female sparrow can sing! If you don't stand up and salute when she performs "God Bless America," I suggest you check your earthly passport because I'm pretty sure it's lapsed. Sandi hits notes a missile couldn't reach, and when they fall back to earth, it's as if they divide into a million messages of cheer to bless the recipients. I've watched celebrated singers move to the edge of their chairs so as not to miss one moment of Sandi's offering. And by the time she's made her way up the musical scale, one stunning octave at a time, stained glass tears of gratitude stream down their faces at not only the expansiveness of her range but also at the privilege of having heard in their lifetimes such an extraordinarily beautiful voice.

While few have Sandi's gift, other melodic sounds cheer us on our way. Take nature. She sings continually, not just through sparrows but also through the contralto voice of the wind in a tree. As I write, autumn taps outside my window. Our massive maple has caught a harmony of breezy notes in her branches and is shaking her head with joy, causing a flurry of leaves to gyrate and curtsy as they tumble toward the ground. And I love the sound of bass drums rumbling deep inside thunder, the wind chime verses composed in morning brooks, and the xylophones created by spattering raindrops as they reverberate off tin roofs and dribble down eaves.

Soon winter's ballads, blues, and bebop will be heard with all their flurry and fury. Her icy breath will ping on windowpanes, her howling complaints will rush down chimneys, and her lullaby silence will fill us with quiet wonder after she's tucked the land under a blanket of snow. Perhaps her frozen notes that somehow warm our souls do so because we have the promise that winter will pass, and with its passing the songbirds will fill our hearts.

> *For behold, the winter is past,*
> *The rain is over and gone.*
> *The flowers have already appeared in the land;*
> *The time has arrived for pruning the vines,*
> *And the voice of the turtledove has been heard in our land.*
>
> (SONG OF SOLOMON 2:11–12)

Yes, nature sings.

And so does my husband.

He sings all the time. If you think that's exaggerating, you haven't met Les. As soon as he could after birth, he sang. When he could stand on his own, he stood on a barrel in his front yard and performed in wait of an audience. And finally he got one.

In fact, "Rudolph the Red-Nosed Reindeer" was his yearly solo at the town hall Christmas play for seven years until Les felt he was too old to croon about a chubby guy and a light-up nose.

Les's school bus driver dubbed him the entertainment crew for their windy rides through the northern woods. Les was full of one-liners and musical verses full of tales. Kind of a "Big Bad John" type of performer, a musical storyteller.

Les's song card is still crammed, but many of his selections remain a bit peculiar as he's drawn to wordy offerings that don't quite make the top ten charts or, for that matter, any charts. People look at me to see if his songs are legitimate or if the ol' boy made them up. But they came out of his years of listening to the static-filled radio in the remote hamlet his family called home. He would gather with his five siblings around the radio as we do a TV football game today and listen to whomever they could tune in. Les also learned some ditties from his alcoholic lumberjack father, who tipped more bottles than birch.

Try these songs on for size: "Olie Svenson, King of the Great North Woods"; "The Heiki Lunda Snow Dance Song"; "The Warship That Landed"; "My Mother the Queen of My Heart"; and "Highway Number Seven" are just a few of the numbers he sings and invites others to join in, which almost no one can. To give you a taste of the first few songs' content, Olie knocks himself in the head with a lead yo-yo; Heiki almost loses his pants in the snow; and a soldier comes home to a broken relationship. From silly songs to sad ones, Les's repertoire runs the musical gamut.

What makes the sparrow sing? We know who made him with that instinct, but why does he sing? I know sometimes it's about mating, but what about the rest of the time? And what makes an abused boy absorb the words of every song that wafts through his broken home and into the cracked places of his heart? What causes one hurt child to never sing and another to never stop?

We know music can create a frenzied feeling, and we also know the serene effect it can enfold folks in, which is why it's played in spas. But what amazes me is the healing power of music and its ability to transport us back through time.

I can't sing one whit. That's been verified by many witnesses. But I love to dance, and as a teenager I attended hops where we did line dances, the twist, the watusi, the chicken, and the waltz (informal). Today all I have to do is hear a few bars of the Tokens singing "The Lion Sleeps Tonight" or Betty Everett belting out "The Shoop, Shoop Song," and I'm catapulted back into yesterday when I'd walk into the school or hall, hoping some cute boy might ask me to dance.

At church when the choir performs "What a Friend" or "In the Garden," I see in my mind's eye my mother singing as she ironed and cleaned. Her songs were especially fervent during storms, as she moved about her tasks with purposed effort.

Mom hadn't always sung around the house. Her songs didn't rise up within her until she experienced the love of Christ. I was nine. I remember. After her encounter with the Lord, she began to sing and then continued to incorporate that lovely habit daily, until Alzheimer's erased the words from the sheets of her mind.

If I could look through the stained glass perspective of music, I believe I would see angels moving the pens of songwriters to create notes of mercy and joy. Words that would help to define us, unite us, ignite our faith, and calm us.

When King Saul was troubled about many things and when he couldn't bear his personal anguish, he would call for David the shepherd boy. The sweet psalmist of Israel had put in many hours on his harp, calming restless sheep and praising his Good Shepherd, so he knew how to soothe a sad heart and acknowledge a good God. The words in David's psalms cover times of peace and war, love and loneliness, and seasons of celebration and disappointment.

From Henry David Thoreau's *Walden*, written more than a century ago, comes this view of troubled souls: "The mass of men lead lives of quiet desperation. What is called resignation is confirmed desperation . . . it is a characteristic of wisdom not to do desperate things." Also from that era "The Voiceless" by Oliver Wendell Holmes: "Alas for those that never sing, but die with all their music in them." Now, I know he wasn't necessarily speaking of a musical composition, but for some, writing in verse has helped them survive a less-than-friendly world.

For the past couple of years, I've had the joy of being on the Women of Faith tour that included Steven Curtis Chapman, his adorable sons, and his darling wife, Mary Beth. Their family went through a great loss that left them emotionally reeling and initially spiritually befuddled. The death of their beloved daughter Maria plunged them into a dark night of struggle. They have been courageous but nonetheless devastated. Out of this cruel season, I've watched the Chapman family find their way back to the song they have been given to sing. The new lyrics have been baptized in their crushing loss. But they don't talk of desperation, Mr. Thoreau. Instead they sing and proclaim destination and reunion. You hear in the words of Steven's latest offerings his tearstained hope, and you sense his determination to sing new words penned from an anguished heart.

The Chapman family has wrestled its way through hard questions and has recognized more fully that not all questions will be answered here on earth. God is under no obligation to explain his ways, and that's not easy for us because we think if we knew the *why*, it would make our loss less brutal and our faith more friendly. The Chapmans avoid offering easy answers to others who hurt and are learning to make greater space for God's mysterious sovereignty.

> By what secret does an ounce of feather and bone produce such music?
>
> —DIANE COOLEDGE PORTER

Have you noticed the songs that bring the most comfort seem to be birthed out of a price we would not willingly pay? I wonder if musically expressed grief helps us to find our way home and guide others as well. Every note a lantern. Every phrase a path.

The path of the house sparrows leads them to gather into

their own neighborhood settings where they join in group activities, which include singing. They have been found chirping in caves (two thousand feet down mine shafts), as well as perched singing atop the observation platform of the Empire State Building. Those feathered Lilliputians get around, and wherever they go, they take their song with them. Well, almost everywhere.

Did you know sparrows have disappeared from central London? The mystery as to why remains unsolved. Even though sizable financial awards have been offered to the one who can figure out their mysterious disappearance, no one has found an answer. Where did they go? Their populous was once as great as the pigeon corps that still flocks on London's streets today.

Perhaps, as in the nursery rhyme about blackbirds, the European birds were baked into pies? Really. A common offering in Britain even after World War I was sparrow pies (probably tasted like chicken). Sometimes at gala affairs, as many as a hundred songbirds would be huddled in a pie. Yikes. Even the thought ruffles my feathers.

What a waste of good music!

Now, what about our music? Are we willing to sing in the darkest night, the deepest pit, or on

> Be like the bird that, passing on her flight awhile on boughs too slight, feels them give way beneath her, and yet sings, knowing that she hath wings.
>
> —VICTOR HUGO

the highest peak? Let's not waste one note of the musical score we've been given.

A Chinese proverb says, "Keep a green tree in your heart, and perhaps a singing bird will come."

How do we maintain a green-tree heart, especially through a blustery winter? I have to remind myself that the life-giving sap is on the inside.

Suggestions:

1. Choose gratitude. If you are in a fresh grief, God isn't offended by your questions and not even by your anger. His love is always greater than our reaction. (Please reread that last sentence.) Even though we're not grateful for our losses—nor should we pretend to be lest the duplicity further fracture our psyches—we can in the midst of it thank God for who he is. It is a sacrifice of praise when we acknowledge his lordship. In return we begin to let go of our perceived rights and rest more fully in his care.

2. Learn to be content not to have all our questions answered. It's a sign of humility and a step toward relinquishment to recognize we aren't in charge, but the One who is accomplishes holy purposes, which don't make sense to us . . . yet.

3. Choose gratitude. Actively being grateful is a conscious choice at first, then with ongoing attentiveness, a habit. It buoys our emotions. Gratitude dissolves anger and untangles the knots inside.

4. Avoid giving easy answers to hard questions that the

hurting ask. We can add to their pain and diminish their hope if we give trite answers to their searching souls. It's okay to admit you don't know what God is up to. Pride can inflate our word count and convince us our value is in persuading others we have answers. Honestly, when I'm hurting, I'd rather have a friend who stands and weeps with me or wonders with me than one who rattles off his or her thin take on the universe.

5. Choose gratitude. Yes, I know I'm repeating myself, but in the midst of hardship, gratitude is the first thing we discard and the first thing we need to recover. It thaws hearts, so our attitudes don't get crusty. It keeps life in perspective and our demands under control. And it protects us from our self-serving tendencies.

Ask God to give you a new song. There is something about singing, especially when you don't feel like it, that mends your heart's tattered wings. It's not a cure-all, but it's a beginning toward recovery for our souls. We are fragile, and when our hearts are shattered, we can't work up a song on our own. God will have to orchestrate it; then it's up to us to sing, sing, sing. It may be a verse from Scripture, a song you've heard before that suddenly becomes personal, or something God's Spirit whispers into your thoughts.

Choose gratitude. Yes, I said it again . . . this time for me. Gratitude is a friend to our inner lives. It freshens our internal atmosphere and spares us from the sinkhole of despair.

Revere God with an attitude of gratitude. Rest in his provisions. Respect others by not being trite. Rejoice with God-breathed lyrics.

God sees a sparrow when he falls, and it matters to the Lord. Imagine that. So how much more will he be attentive to us, his dearly beloved children, in our fallings and failings?

> A bird doesn't sing because it has an answer, it sings because it has a song.
>
> —MAYA ANGELOU

I watched my husband when a hummingbird hit our picture window and knocked himself silly. Les gently picked up the bird and held it between his hands, giving it safe refuge and warmth. Talk about a stained glass spectacle, this tiny, feathered creation, with his iridescent coloring, took our breath away. Pretty soon the bird twitched, and its little wings fluttered. Before long he flew to a nearby wall, where he sat for a long while, as if pondering, and then suddenly he flew off (without so much as a thank-you). Observing Les's tenderness and his supervising care reminded me of God's close attention to our dilemmas. I wonder if we're always aware of his hand and heart for us?

The Art Gallery

Painting: A favorite old watercolor print that pleases me is of a line of birds perched on a stone wall, being taught how to sing by a childlike angel with wand in hand. I don't know the name of this whimsical piece, but I think it would make an endearing stained glass window for a nursery. How lovely to grow up in the glow of knowing the One who delights in pressing songs into our hearts, just as surely as he designed the sparrow to sing.

Museum: *Berlin Museum*. During Flemish baroque painter Peter Paul Rubens's career (1600s) he painted *Child with a Bird*, one of my favorites of his work. The bold piece is done in oil on a dark background; yet with all that intensity, the child is full of innocence. Perhaps the bird is teaching this cherub-faced child to sing? See what you think.

Music: Speaking of songbirds, Nicole C. Mullen singing "Redeemer" is my all-time favorite heart booster, followed by "Call on Jesus." Also when I feel low, I listen to her sing "Forever You Reign," which is another reminder that stirs celebration. These are hand-raising, toe-tapping, joy-bringing songs to help us get our happy on.

Mandisa singing "The Voice of a Savior" makes me want to rise up and carry on. And have you heard her sing "He Is with You"? Well, I have, about one hundred times, and it's still not enough.

"Can't Live a Day" by Avalon is on my top-ten list of favorite songs. If it doesn't lift your spirits, I'll foot for a cup of java. Yes, it's that good. Thanks, Janna, for singing those words into the depth of my need.

Poem: "The Silence" by Wendell Berry. Poems are meant to be pondered. Sit with the words, soak them up, speak them aloud, write down the lines or phrases you like best, and lastly, share them with someone. The more of your senses that you involve in a poem, the greater the heart ownership becomes, and who couldn't use some added beauty in their souls?

Scripture: "Are not five sparrows sold for two farthings, and not one of them is forgotten before God? But even the very hairs of your head are all numbered. Fear not therefore: ye are of more value than many sparrows." (Luke 12:6–7 KJV)

> *It is a good thing to give thanks unto the LORD, and to sing*
> *praises unto thy name, O most High.*
>
> (PSALM 92:1 KJV)

> *Oh come, let us sing to the LORD!*
> *Let us shout joyfully to the Rock of our salvation.*
> *Let us come before His presence with thanksgiving;*
> *Let us shout joyfully to Him with psalms.*
>
> (PSALM 95:1–2 NKJV)

Chapter 6

Stained Glass
Prayer

Was it training, respect, or longing that caused Old Testament Daniel to open his window every day toward Jerusalem when he prayed? Or as is true in life, is the answer all three? Often I find that my motives are usually layered.

For instance, take church. I attend because I was taught at a young age I should go. I attend because I long for fellowship with other believers. And I go because I believe it's a way to respect God. Oh, wait, did I mention guilt? Yes, I've gone because I felt that God and his people might think less of me if I didn't. Perhaps because some of them have told me so.

A church in my neighborhood left its doors unlocked as a gesture to the public to come and to seek refuge quietly in their stained glass sanctuary. An open invitation to pray. I found it settling to stop in and had visited on a number of occasions. In fact, even though I was alone, I could hear music as I sat quietly. It might have been from my memories of years of churchgoing; it could have been from my heart, where God has been writing new lyrics for me to sing; or maybe it was the sparrows in the small courtyard outside the church doors; but whatever the source, it was lovely.

Recently ruffians robbed the generous, tiny church, causing the congregants to rethink their open-door policy. And causing me to rethink my safety. I haven't been back since. Sad how enemies take us captive through intimidation.

As I pondered the lionhearted Daniel, I observed his stout heart in the midst of his enemies. I wondered if I had been a captive, even one in an influential position, would I have been so faithful to pray with Daniel's frequency, fervency, and gratitude, despite threats? Actually, I think I know the answer.

> In his [Daniel's] upper room, with his windows open toward Jerusalem, he knelt down on his knees three times that day, and prayed and gave thanks before his God, as was his custom since early days.
>
> —DANIEL 6:10 NKJV

I recently was a "captive" on an airplane that was parked on the tarmac for almost two hours, waiting for permission to leave. While I prayed fervently for my release, I must admit my gratitude was nil. All I could think about was how complicated this delay was going to make my day. I could see freedom out my window, as I had a view of the terminal, but I couldn't convince anyone to let me go. Two hours of inconvenience within miles from home, and I whined internally the whole time, compared to Daniel, who lived a lifetime as a stranger in a foreign land and continued to offer up a sacrifice of praise.

When Daniel threw open his window coverings, the view was of his captive land surrounding him. Homes filled with jealous enemies crowded in like so many militant soldiers. Yet Daniel purposed to dismiss that perspective and, with a grateful heart, direct his thoughts toward home and his visionary prayers toward Jehovah. I wonder if sparrows and doves came to his window and sang songs from his homeland?

I don't do well in hostile environments. Why is it some folks such as Daniel flourish spiritually in the midst of dissension? While, truth be known, I can wilt at the first signs of others' displeasure. I guess I'm too tied to others' opinions, rely too much on their approval, and have at times allowed others' treatment to define my worth. I want people to like me, and when they don't, I feel defensive and insecure. I allow those two emotional jailers to keep me locked out of gratitude and locked into my ragtag humanity.

I note in the beginning of Daniel's story (in Daniel 1) he was an exceptional young man. Well, it really wasn't the beginning of his story because we don't have access in Scripture to details regarding the specifics of his childhood, but we are introduced to him as a teenager. He is a Jewish lad taken captive by the Babylonians. He was chosen by his enemies for his intelligence, character, and good looks.

Wow! What would they have done with me? As a teen I was loud, moody, and rebellious. Besides that, my looks were complicated by an ever-changing array of hairdos from the fifties: ponytails, beehives, and flips. My coifs alone would have been enough to get me locked up. I think I might have been a throw-away-the-key type of captive. But not Daniel. He was definitely a keeper destined for greatness. It pays to behave . . . but not always in the ways we imagine.

You would think with Daniel's squeaky-clean behavior that he would have deserved an easy existence. That's the way we think, isn't it? A friend recently told me that upon hearing the news of a family member being diagnosed with cancer, the first words out of his mouth were, "Why her? She's the one who sings in the choir, teaches Sunday school, takes care of the sick and the elderly. She didn't deserve this."

It's human nature to think that if we do right, all good things will come our way. Yet we could each jot down a list of good people who have suffered greatly. What's that about?

My dear friend Carol would have been the name on the top of my she-didn't-deserve-a-hard-life list. Carol had a kind heart and a loving, inclusive spirit toward all. She was a wonderful artist, cook, and a devoted grandmother. Yet she suffered traumatic losses and lingering physical challenges that eventually took her life. She still had great art inside of her, waiting to get out, and vats of love to pour on her family. Then there are those who bring nothing to the table, treat others with malice, and commit despicable crimes; so why not them? Leave the Carols; take the bad guys.

It's human to wonder and wrestle. Give yourself permission to pray your doubts and despair. God isn't offended by our frailty. No one knows better than God that we are dust.

There's no denying it: we live in a fallen world, and no one gets out of it without suffering. Some greatly. The Fall left distortions in our windowpanes, our viewing places, our perspectives. So perhaps we have to learn to do what Daniel did when he focused his vision on Jehovah and prayed . . . every day . . . three times a day.

I'm not suggesting this is a formula to avoid bad things happening to good people. We can see in Daniel's story that although he survived his enemies, he still was criticized, plotted against, and lied about. Prayer doesn't necessarily rescue us from all evil intentions or diabolical schemes, but instead it gives us a resource for comfort, wisdom, strength, and unexplainable joy in the midst of the ravenous lions of life. And when we lose our joy, the Spirit replaces it with endurance, that indestructible, internal insistence to keep on keeping on.

I pray every day. My prayers usually are conversational, ones in which I talk to the Lord and he kindly listens. Sometimes I sense his presence; other times I pray in faith, believing in what I can't see or feel. I pray for people in my life, for some more than others. At times I shoot emergency requests like arrows, hoping to pierce the compassion of Christ. And sometimes I sit silently and wait for God's Spirit to counsel me. I wish I were better at that kind of prayer because during those times I gain the ability to survive the injustices and inequities of this life with more grace and holy ingenuity. I've noticed the more acute my ear becomes to identifying the Lord's voice from the ongoing racket in my head, the more sensitive and discriminating my "knower" is.

The first book I remember being placed in my hands as a child was a Golden Book of prayers. Later as a young adult and a new child of God, my first grown-up book on prayer was by O. Hallesby. I think it ironic that today I live across the street from where I am told Hallesby preached for a time. That thought delights me. It also may explain why so many people in the neighborhood are believers. I can just imagine Hallesby in prayer, claiming the town for Christ.

> To pray is nothing more involved than to open the door, giving Jesus access to our needs and permitting Him to exercise His own power in dealing with them.
>
> —O. HALLESBY

Today the church he attended is gone and a smaller, multicultural church stands in its place. On Sunday mornings during fair weather, the congregation leaves the doors open, and the music and praise fill my porch and waft through the neighborhood. I think the preacher whose ministry was hallmarked by prayer would be pleased.

Many great books on prayer are on the market by folks such as Hallesby, Foster, and Yancey that can help answer our unspoken questions on this sometimes ethereal topic. Of course, David's songs, journal entries, and prayers in the Psalms are a great place to listen in on the angst of a struggling heart. Talk about mood swings and injustice; David has been there and done that. Yet, as far as we know, he never retired his harp or halted his worship, even when his infant son died. David had stayed on his face before the Lord, praying and fasting for the life of his child, until word came the baby had died. Then David rose up, washed his tearstained face, and carried on with his life.

That isn't to say he didn't grieve, but once David knew the outcome, he seemed to have the courage to accept it as part of God's baffling yet sovereign plan. I believe that even though David learned to breathe deeply again, he walked out the rest of his life with a shard of pain in his heart, inscribed with that baby's name across it. A long song of sorrow nested within him that colored his heart with mercy and his memories with regret. That's just how loss impacts humanity. We carry on; we never forget. Not a baby . . . ever.

After the death of Papaw, my grandmother, whom we called Mamaw, lived alone as a widow for thirty-five years. She carried on. Her dependence on prayer to companion her, to calm her, and to protect her were inspiring. Mamaw's spiritual commitment guided her gait throughout

> Surely the goodness of God has been the same to us as to the saints of old. Let us, then, weave His mercies into a song . . . Let our souls give forth music as sweet and as exhilarating as came from David's harp, as we praise the Lord whose mercy endures forever.
>
> —CHARLES SPURGEON

her years and then into God's presence. She loved church, radio preaching, singing old hymns, reading her Bible, and praying. A cracker crumb never passed Mamaw's lips without first a word of thanksgiving to the Lord. She was disciplined, neat as a pin, and quite proper. There would be breaks in her reserve when she would get "happy in the Lord." Then you would see joy light up her deep creases; she would clap her vein-drenched hands and tap her narrow foot with the spiritual vigor of a young woman.

Mamaw married Papaw when she was very young, and they went on to have four children. She lived to bury them all. I can't begin to understand the impact of that kind of multiple loss; yet she wasn't a woman given to complaints or despair. She seemed to have a determined heart, a David heart, to live out her life and losses with poise.

One of my favorite memories of Mamaw was when she would drag the wooden kitchen chair to the window, pull out her big-print Bible and a magnifying glass, and sit to read her Sunday school lesson with her bifocals tenaciously perched on her nose. Mamaw read each word in whispers and pored over them like newly discovered photos of her family. She would tip her face into the warmth of the sunlight, close her cataract-veiled eyes, and repeat God's words into her prayers.

My grandmother's simple life and faith are profound for me today. Maybe I'm more aware now that I'm more seasoned of how much she did without and how much grief and loneliness she bore in her lifetime. She had very little in earthly possessions, although she didn't seem to concern herself with things, for her affections were firmly fixed on Jesus. She didn't want you to buy her anything, but she treasured visits, letters, pictures, and conversations about the Lord.

Mamaw's life spanned ninety-seven and a half years, from horse-and-buggy days to freeways to men-taking-giant-steps-on-the-moon days. She watched the world change dramatically, and she watched her personal lifescape shift in ways she couldn't have anticipated. I still remember hearing my dad negotiate with Mamaw, his mom, to convince her to upgrade from an icebox to a refrigerator and later from a radio to the addition of a small television. If he thought his bargaining talents were stretched then, it was nothing compared to coaxing her to give up her "chamber pot" for the newly installed "water closet" on the back porch.

> The beloved of the Lord are to hand down their witness for the gospel, and the covenant to their heirs, and these again to their next descendants . . . We are to begin at the family hearth.
>
> —CHARLES SPURGEON

But some things in her life remained the same: Mamaw lived in her little four-room house (five hundred square feet) on East Broadway almost her entire life, and she never wavered in following Christ—the last being her greatest legacy.

One way we can extend our legacy and increase its richness for future generations is to write out and leave our prayers. That's what Christian Reisner did. Who's he? I wish I could say he, too, was a relative, but honestly I didn't know him in person. Yet I do feel as if I know him in spirit through his prayers published in 1909. I discovered this wee, two-by-three-and-a-half-inch volume in an antique store more than twenty years ago when I reluctantly paid $1.50 to own it. Today *Week-Day Prayers* is among my most precious possessions. His prayer offerings are short yet richly infused with meaning that never fail to resonate within me. He wrote them as if he wanted us to pause and meditate on each word. Listen in . . .

O Thou Tender Shepherd, straighten all our paths today. Save us from the hesitation of doubt. Make us considerate of others' feelings. Soften the sharp words that threaten to slip off our tongues. Sweeten our deeds with kindness. Teach us how, like our Lord, to endure wrong in silence. Ballast us with love. Direct our aims. Steady our hearts. Plant right loves. Employ our good impulses. Give direction to enthusiasm. Spur us to our best. Bring us to the end with our assigned tasks well done.

May I suggest you now reread this prayer, pausing after each sentence. Then read it aloud and notice what phrases stick to your soul. Words that give us pause are often a window to our needs. We collect up life so quickly that we sprint past aches residing inside of us—tucked in the corners—that long to be addressed. Sticky words can open skylights of understanding.

While I'm drawn to the simplicity and brevity of Reisner's

prayers, some seasons I find my soul in need of the lush pasture of Charles Spurgeon's writings. His devotions in *Morning and Evening* remain classic words so powerfully woven that I often speak them into my own prayers.

We were designed to pray—whether short or long, simple or complex—by the very fact that our internal default is to cry out to God. When we're at the end of our ropes, it's a human response to implore in a whisper, a shout, or a tremble from our interior, "Oh, God, help me." And many a life conversion has transpired in just that manner.

"Oh, God, help me" remains a powerful way to begin and end our prayers. Holy bookends. Four words that say, "I acknowledge you, God, and I recognize my need of you."

My friend Ian gave me a circle of prayer beads, like a bracelet, meant to help with concentration and memorization. He told me to choose a Scripture for each bead, then to pray the verses every day for as long as it takes to make them truly mine. Then whenever I chose, I could add a few new verses, names of people, or printed prayers. I find lines from David's psalms or lines from a hymn are often fitting.

Even though prayer beads are outside my experience, tradition, and comfort zone, I've found they help me to stay mentally on track because I tend to be easily distracted. Like Winnie the Pooh, I have fluff in my brain. And may I say, the older I get, the fluffier I become, leaving me susceptible to every passing breeze? But these glass orbs, when fingered, keep me attentive to my story of faith.

Once the beads became a part of my morning prayers, I found even to hold them reminded me not only to quiet myself before the Lord, but also of God's circle of protection around my life. I must say, that kind of prompt in this dangerous world is comforting.

There are many ways to pray. You might pray like Daniel, three times a day, or like my grandmother, at a window with your face warmed by the sun, or while in a dark closet, prison cell, or hospital bed. You might pray free-form, spilling out the detailed contents of your heart, or structured, succinct, or with groans. Style doesn't matter. Participation does. Lean in, listen, and respond.

Oh, God, help me. Amen.

PS. I think I'll stop by that church in town to see if the door is unlocked.

The Art Gallery ———————————————

Museums: In *Chiesa di Santa Maria del Popolo* in Rome, Italy, stands a sculpture of Daniel by Bernini that's stirring. Done in the baroque style, note how the artist captured young Daniel's passionate plea toward Jehovah God.

The National Gallery, Washington, DC. In the 1600s the Flemish artist Sir Peter Paul Rubens painted that masterpiece of Daniel in the lions' den. If you study it carefully, it will make the hair on your arms quiver. Look at the lions' faces. Is it my imagination or are several of them staring out at us? Their fierceness is in contrast to Daniel's meek, heavenly gaze. Next time the "lions" are about to get you, remember this stunning visual. No matter how intimidating the enemy, God is stronger yet.

National Gallery, London, England. The Virgin in Prayer by Giovanni Battista Salvi da Sassoferrato, an Italian baroque painter, is an exquisite oil rendition of Mary. The colors are vivid and strong while Mary is tender yet resolute.

Prayer: "The Merton Prayer" was written by Thomas Merton and has been repeated and reproduced so regularly, it's become known by this simple name. In it Merton expresses how he has no idea where he is going but he knows what he desires to do as he moves forward. It's a wonderful reminder of what's important as we take the long view of life. To read it, Google "The Merton Prayer."

Whenever I find my heart stopped by a passage in the Bible, a verse in a poem, a picture in a book, or a phrase in a story, I have learned to pause and ask, "Is God speaking to me through this?" I don't want to rush past something that holds significance for my life, although I'm sure I have many times. Any heart-spark can be the kindling for prayer and revelation. Here are a couple that fired up my thoughts.

- "God does not send us despair in order to kill us; he sends it in order to awaken us to new life."—*Reflections* by Hermann Hesse

I would pray this by confessing, "Lord, I trust your motives regarding my welfare. I believe you have my best interests in mind. May my despair awaken within me new life, for without you in the midst, my soul withers. Amen."

- I love these lines: "I want to beg you to be patient toward all that is unsolved in your heart and to try to love the questions themselves like locked rooms and like books that are written in a very foreign tongue."
—*Letters to a Young Poet* by Rainer Maria Rilke

    I would pray this by saying, "Lord, I long to be patient with all that is unsolved within me, but I'll need your assistance. Teach me to love the questions that stomp around in my head while I wait for you to unlock answers within me. I rest in the fact that you are often a mystery, and I am made in your image. Amen."

Music: "A Mighty Fortress Is Our God" penned by Martin Luther in 1529. Every once in a while I like to pull out a hymnal (purchased at an old bookstore, not heisted from church, thank you), go through the songs, and read the verses aloud. So many are tender, powerful, and poignant. Have you thought about the words from "A Mighty Fortress Is Our God" recently? The third verse reads:

And though this world, with devils filled,
should threaten to undo us,
we will not fear, for God hath willed
his truth to triumph through us.
The Prince of Darkness grim,
we tremble not for him;
his rage we can endure,
for lo, his doom is sure;
one little word shall fell him.

"Be Still and Know That He Is God," Steven Curtis Chapman;
"Sanctus," Travis Cottrell; "A Mighty Fortress Is Our God,"
Sheila Walsh

Scripture: "Give thanks unto the LORD, call upon his name,
make known his deeds among the people." (I Chronicles 16:8 KJV)

I will remember the deeds of the LORD;
yes, I will remember your miracles of long ago.

(PSALM 77:11 NIV)

He who offers a sacrifice of thanksgiving honors Me;
And to him who orders his way aright
I shall show the salvation of God.

(PSALM 50:23)

For the LORD *is a great God, and a great King above all gods.*

In his hand are the deep places of the earth: the strength of the hills is his
    also.

The sea is his, and he made it: and his hands formed the dry land.

O come, let us worship and bow down: let us kneel before the LORD *our*
    maker.

(PSALM 95:3–6 KJV)

Chapter 7

Wisps of Poetry from Stained Glass Hearts

Please don't skip this chapter if poetry isn't your thing, if you find it boring or unnecessary in the big dreams and great schemes of the universe. I promise not to dump my own poetic graphite shavings into the mix. Unless I'm overtaken by angelic inspiration and can't hold myself back . . . then quickly flip to the next chapter.

Poetry and prayer could be sisters, playmates, or at least BFFs (best friends forever). For both often contain thoughts on joy, anguish, uncertainty, anger, fear, courage, love, and loss. Both can come from a searching heart, a dither of disillusionment, or a sense of placement.

> Your prayer can be poetry, and poetry can be your prayer.
>
> —TERRI GUILLEMETS

Both poetry and prayer help us to express and to expose the insecurities and substance of our humanity. If we're attentive, in the midst of them we will hear chatty angels on assignment.

Fanny Crosby penned it thus in her hymn "Blessed Assurance":

Angels descending, bring from above,
Echoes of mercy, whispers of love.

And listen to Pixie Foudre:

Browsing the dim back corner
Of a musty antique shop
Opened an old book of poetry
Angels flew out from the pages
I caught the whiff of a soul
The ink seemed fresh as today
Was that voices whispering?
The tree of the paper still grows.

I love every line of Pixie's poem. Read it again. Please. It's so full of life. Besides, a well-written piece is worthy of rereads so that it settles solidly in the heart. From the browsing to the whispers, I'm intrigued by the picture Foudre has painted. Who among us hears enough love whispers during our short jaunt around our rocky planet? Plus, I've experienced angels pouring forth from ancient pages; haven't you? Oh, not angels I could see, but I felt the wind from their wings on my fluttering heart when lines rose off the pages and filled me with the sweet incense of truth.

Poetry captures wisps of our hearts, half-formed thoughts that, when fully expressed, lend themselves to our settling more comfortably into our own skin, much like sinking into a down-filled chair as it surrounds us with assurance. When working on his glass art, my husband finds that with every piece added to his pattern, the project becomes more complete, more understood. That's how it is with partial lines penned from our hearts that fill in the pattern of our lives, making it more understandable as it's exposed to the light.

Of course, not all poetry is comforting. Some is brutal, raging, prejudicial, and caustic. I don't purpose to go down dangerous alleys because I find life already offers me enough threat of violence; I don't need to seek it out in any form. Instead, I'm longing for a "road less traveled." Give me an insight inscribed on a butterfly's breath, a thought spun in gossamer across a windowpane, a witty saying in script on the underbelly of a ladybug. Ugly is smeared on enough windows; I want a view of cumulus eruptions, luminous spires, and firefly extravaganzas. I want lines worthy of my grandchildren's attention from generation to generation.

So what is a poem? Listen to a few great poets, like slivers of stained glass thoughts, as they define their life work.

- "A poem begins as a lump in the throat, a sense of wrong, a homesickness, a lovesickness."—Robert Frost
- "Out of the quarrel with others we make rhetoric; out of the quarrel with ourselves we make poetry."—W. B. Yeats
- "Poetry . . . should strike the reader as a wording of his own highest thoughts, and appear almost a remembrance."—John Keats

- "Poetry is a deal of joy and pain and wonder, with a dash of the dictionary."—Kahlil Gibran
- "Poetry is a packsack of invisible keepsakes."—Carl Sandburg
- And my favorite: "Genuine poetry can communicate before it is understood."—T. S. Eliot

Poetry, according to the dictionary, when brought down to its most common denominator is "expressed feelings and ideas set to a rhythm." Rhythms that we first experience as raindrops on a windowsill, a squeaking rocking chair lulling us to sleep, our mother's patterned hum as she tends to life. Then we learn as children in the nursery to recite verses about blackbirds in a pie, a wife in a pumpkin shell, cows in the corn, and a baby in the treetop.

Poetry from the beginning seemed to be about being in something: in trouble, in love, in heartache, in recovery, in confusion, and so forth. The musical meter helped us to memorize lines quickly and repeat them at will. As we grew, so did the types of poems that spoke to our souls or strummed on our funny bones.

Sometimes rhymes are ticklish, like Shel Silverstein's work, "Hug O' War": "I will not play tug o' war. I'd rather play hug o' war."

And playful like Dr. Seuss in *Happy Birthday to You*: "There is no one alive who is Youer than You."

Sometimes written verses are full of passion, as in

Shakespeare's *Midsummer Night's Dream,* or haunting, like Edgar Allen Poe's poem "The Raven." Many poems become songs ("The Twelve Days of Christmas"), ballads, hymns, and prayers of grace, like the one that hangs on my kitchen wall (the words were written by John Cennick in the mid-1700s):

> *Be present at our table, Lord;*
> *Be here, as everywhere adored.*
> *These mercies bless and grant that we*
> *May feast in paradise with Thee.*
> *Amen.*

Some poetry even becomes epitaphs. This quirky one is carved on a gravestone at Winterborn Steepleton Cemetery in Dorsetshire, England:

> *Here lies the body*
> *Of Margaret Bent*
> *She kicked up her heels*
> *And away she went.*

That makes me giggle. I wonder if, early on, Margaret penned her high-stepping rhyme as she grinned over a steaming cup of huckleberry tea, or if she truly sprinted away so quickly that someone else—an old beau, perhaps—thought the rhyme captured her lively nature and speedy departure.

Epitaphs remind me of Internet messages in which you

are limited to 140 characters or less, which means you'd better hurry and get to the point. That was accomplished in a Nova Scotia cemetery where a headstone boasted:

Here lies Ezekial Aikle. Age 102. The good die young.

Well, that leaves us pondering. Did Ezekial stay young all his life, or was he proof that ornery folks tend to stick around?

The poems I chase after are ones that go to deep places, awaken me with truth, and calm me with beauty. Those include the ones that catch me off guard with laughter, those that allow me to be a child again, or those that cause me to relive a magical moment. Some of my favorite poets are Luci Shaw, A. A. Milne, and Ken Gire.

Recently Jan Silvious, friend and author, shared with me her appreciation of Ella Wheeler Wilcox. I realized that while the poet's lines were familiar, I didn't know her name.

Laugh, and the world laughs with you;
Weep, and you weep alone.
For the sad old earth must borrow its mirth,
But has trouble enough of its own.
Sing, and the hills will answer;
Sigh, it is lost on the air.
The echoes bound to a joyful sound,
But shrink from voicing care.

Rejoice, and men will seek you;
Grieve, and they turn and go.
They want full measure of all your pleasure,
But they do not need your woe.
Be glad, and your friends are many;
Be sad, and you lose them all.
There are none to decline your nectared wine,
But alone you must drink life's gall.
Feast, and your halls are crowded;
Fast, and the world goes by.
Succeed and give, and it helps you live,
But no man can help you die.
There is room in the halls of pleasure
For a long and lordly train,
But one by one we must all file on
Through the narrow aisles of pain.

(ELLA WHEELER WILCOX, "SOLITUDE")

I suggest reading this one over regularly. I plan on it.

For some reason, I thought today's society as a whole had lost touch with the poet in them, but then I Googled the word *poetry*, and the results showed that more than eighty-two million sites existed. Eighty-two million. I guess I shouldn't be surprised that in this fractured world, with its dank corners and mysterious beliefs, people are looking for a way, a window, to call out and express what troubles them and what sustains them. Since the world was created full of rhythms like the waves of the sea, cycles of the moon, and return of the monarchs and swallows, it would only follow the Creator's pattern that we, too, would be rhythmic in expression.

Speaking of nature, it's an endless palette of inspiration for the sage.

He will not see me stopping here
To watch his woods fill up with snow.
(ROBERT FROST, FROM "STOPPING BY WOODS
ON A SNOWY EVENING")

I wish I could see how the ocean is lashing
The foam of its billows to whirlwinds of spray;
I wish I could see how its proud waves are dashing,
And hear the wild roar of their thunder to-day!
(ANNE BRONTË, FROM "LINES COMPOSED IN
A WOOD ON A WINDY DAY")

Something sacramental speaks
in the rinsing of hard stone by mountain run-off.
(LUCI SHAW, FROM *Writing the River*)

Many of us have come to love the ones who have left lovely lines that fit inside us, poetry that helps us to see our world more grandly and ourselves more kindly. I love Emily Dickinson. Even though I never met her in person, I've met her in heart. Historians say she was a recluse and toward the end of her life never left her room. As a former agoraphobic, I get that. But I'm so grateful that God gave her heart wings to take her emotionally beyond her bedroom window and to pen her thoughts so eloquently. I'm glad her words didn't wither inside her.

Not everyone leaves a written legacy. My parents held in their lives, like Houdini held in his breath as he struggled free from the knots of chains that bound him. By the time my mom and dad finally exhaled, they left this life with much unspoken (which wasn't unusual for their generation). My mother's childhood was mostly a secret society only she and her sisters and brothers were members of, so I missed out on the details that made her the determined woman she became. My dad wasn't much of a talker, so he left the words up to the womenfolk of his life, which means I barely have a sketch of his growing-up years and young adult life.

My dad's mom was very proper and didn't believe in sharing with anyone. My mom's mother died when Mom was a child, and her dad died before I was born. My papaw died when I was nine, and he was by far the quietest man I had ever met. In fact, I have no memory of his voice. He once gave me a nickel that he dug out—with fingers stained by chewing tobacco—of the corner of his change purse and placed in my tiny, white hand. That might have been our only exchange.

It went many years,
But at last came a knock,
And I thought of the door

With no lock to lock.
I blew out the light,
I tip-toed the floor,
And raised both hands
In prayer to the door.
But the knock came again.
My window was wide;
I climbed on the sill
And descended outside.
Back over the sill
I bade a "Come in"
To whatever the knock
At the door may have been.
So at a knock
I emptied my cage
To hide in the world
And alter with age.

(Robert Frost, "The Lockless Door")

Everyone interprets meaning through his or her own grid, regardless of where the poet was actually coming from or intending to go. That's part of the glory of a poem; it fits inside of us often according to our need. Or perhaps we are just so self-serving and desperate for answers that we wring words dry, trying to fill our own cups. All that to say, for me, Frost's night visitor's tapping was his "secrets," which are harder to repress as one ages. To maintain his denial and escape his fears of the truth, he slips out the window and continues to pretend who he is rather than say what is true. Others interpret the visitor to be death. There are those who believe his depression is rapping while others interpret it as yet something else. For me, in the mind-set of my family, "secrets" fits.

How I wish at least one of my relatives had left behind a scrap, a written trace of his or her life . . . journals, letters, poems. There is an inborn need to know our people that goes past inquisitiveness. The more we know about our families, the more it seems to help us understand ourselves. A poem can open the stained glass window of the heart to help us see into the story of another and read our own more accurately. It broadens our perspectives. Sometimes written words feel safer to speak to a papered line than to risk words spoken into the ear of uncertainty.

I recently found a book of poems in my mother's belongings. It had two dog-eared pages that I have scoured, as one searching for a path home, wondering which lines captured her attention or defined her feelings. I wish she would have underlined a phrase, dashed off a thought in the margins, or even dated it.

> In three words I can sum up everything I've learned about life: it goes on.
>
> —ROBERT FROST

Bread crumbs. Be generous. Leave some.

While my folks didn't know the importance of leaving behind even crumbs, I do. I can choose to grieve forever over what my family didn't give (and they gave much in other ways), or I can busy myself giving what I can. It's often from what we didn't receive that we learn how to give something meaningful to others. So I have scribbled my thoughts in books, poems, half-written journals, quotes, letters, and on endless scraps of paper.

Does my family need all that? Nope. Excess is always, well, excessive. I guess I needed purging. Or maybe I thought I had to speak for my silent family. No one will do this life exactly right, but I promise you that a box full of poems, even if they aren't ones you wrote but that you prized; a bundle of letters you did write; a book with your commentary in the margins will become a treasure chest for someone to finger through on cold nights to warm him or her.

> Each man carries within him the soul of a poet who died young.
>
> —SAINTE-BEUVE

In a bookstore's overflow garage full of used tomes, I recently unearthed an old composition book with handwritten notes in English and French on literature, art, poets, music, and Christ's life. If topically set into a window, it would be luminous. The bookstore owner, seeing the delight I took in this overlooked piece, gave it to me as a gift. I rushed home to peruse it. The script is meticulous, and the outlines are detailed. At first I thought it to be a woman's hand, but it may be a man's flourished writing. Even though I don't know the person, I value the effort, and I'm thoroughly enjoying it. The person's words haven't been wasted and, in fact, are being shared.

The Art Gallery

Poems: *"I Wandered Lonely as a Cloud" by William Wordsworth.* If it's been a while since you've read this one or if you've never been introduced to it, don't miss the daffodil dance. Allow the word pictures to fill you with wonder and praise. The title sounds a tad dismal while the poem is sheer delight.

Can you think of a lasting visual that you could pen a few words about and leave as a trace for your family? It doesn't have to be grand; besides, if you've never tried a poetic tilt to your perspective, you might find you like the view.

"The Swan" by Mary Oliver. Oliver has written some wonderful lines in her poem. The birds' descriptions are breathtaking as she allows you to sit in the night with the silhouetted swan and then rise with it at dawn. It looks like "an armful of white blossoms, a perfect commotion of silk and linen."

I read this poem regularly. I keep it on my desktop, and it never fails to please my senses. At the end of the poem is a question that I hope you'll ponder.

Museum: *The Neue Pinakothek* (New Pinakothek) in Munich, which houses many works by one of my favorite artists, Carl Spitzweg.

Artist: *Carl Spitzweg.* One of my new discoveries is a painting by Carl Spitzweg from 1839 called *The Poor Poet*. It depicts the hard life of a struggling writer. It's charming, and even though you can feel the chill on the poet's bones as he is huddled under his tattered umbrella and meager blanket, you also sense his devotion to his papers and books. Obviously he's willing to sacrifice to press his thoughts into existence. (I wish I had the subject's address. I'd high-step it right over there, swishing a pot of potato soup, chamomile tea, and a goose down comforter. Oh, yes, and carrying a basket of apple logs for his fire. But then I'd wreck the whole scene.)

Spetzweg was a chemist, a self-taught painter, and yes, a poet. No wonder he captured the poor chap in his painting so well. Oh, that we might all struggle long enough to understand the disenfranchised and then live long enough and honorably enough to give them visibility.

Spetzweg also did a painting of a saint, one of a stargazer, one of a man reading in a field, another one in a park . . . all with a whimsical touch. I love this man!

Scripture: For beautiful, picturesque poetry read Psalms and Song of Solomon.

Chapter 8

Stained Glass Books

I'm often between two books, sandwiched, like a ham and cheese on rye. And not just books of poetry. Oh, no. Books from many genres are my lunch companions, my pillow companions, and my travel companions. I have books everywhere in my home. I decorate with them, I give them as gifts, I admire them, and I honestly read them. I have a true passion for the ownership and perusal of said tomes. I even have statues, decorator pillows, and framed art featuring stacks of books and people reading. If it were up to me, I would mandate people to wear pages of great books as clothing (copies, of course). Then no one would be boring.

Think of it. If a conversation went the way of the Sahara, one could pipe in fresh water by reading a sleeve or two, quoting a collar, or scanning a shoe. Well, you get the idea.

I can't talk about my own journey without focusing on my passion for books and encouraging you to become a full-fledged reader, if you're not already. My road to recovery was paved with volumes of books. When something changes in your life, it's hard not to shout about it from the rooftop in hopes it will do the same for others. For one thing, books, more often than I'm willing to own, have rescued me from my mood-soaked self.

Malachi 3:10 says, "I will . . . open for you the windows of heaven and pour out for you a blessing until it overflows." I enjoy thinking of those windows as stained glass ones representing our redeemed lives; the windows are ajar so angels can pour out blessed thoughts into the hearts of humanity to be written into books. That visual pleases me. That's not the correct interpretation of the verse since it has to do with tithes, but as a writer with an active imagination and need for divine intervention, I like it. I'm sure "the windows of heaven" will be beyond human description. Maybe they'll be stained glass holograms? Whoa.

Until then I love that when we read fine books, they can nudge open the windows of our hearts so we might become better partners, parents, employees, and friends. I find it feels safer to take truth in during private reading times at home than, say, sitting in a lecture with 250 other people. Besides, the decision to read keeps verve in our vocabulary, ignites color in our imaginations, and boosts our underchallenged brains, giving them something to do besides holding up our hats.

> O Day of days when we can read! The reader and the book, either without the other is naught.
>
> —RALPH WALDO EMERSON

God used books to help fill in my gaping education, heal my bruised emotions, and improve my relational exchanges.

They became not only my tutors but also at times my medication. Books can transport us to places beyond our usual travels; we can plunge to undersea colonies, skydive into remote villages, and blast off into outer space while still safely tethered to the living room sofa. Seat belts advised.

Speaking of space, have you read Madeleine L'Engle's *A Wrinkle in Time*? It's a grown-up children's fantasy book that takes the reader on a thrilling science adventure. For some time Madeleine couldn't find a publisher interested in this piece. They declared it to be "outside the box" of normal. Today it has won many prestigious awards, including the Newbery, and is required reading in most schools. So much for boxes—and "normal."

I love stories about authors and their circuitous routes to fame because we tend to assume that classics were embraced instantly and the writer celebrated. Not necessarily so. I'm grateful that Madeleine lived long enough to be aware of the impact she had on readers with not only this book but also with many others.

Beatrix Potter is an author who didn't initially find any publishing enthusiasm for her children's books. Today you would be hard-pressed in our country to find a child who doesn't know Peter Rabbit, Benjamin Bunny, and Squirrel Nutkin. Beloved and treasured, Miss Potter's gentle stories have captured hearts for decades.

If you are a hit-and-miss reader, I recommend starting with some good children's books. Honest. It's a great way to fall in love with reading. If you're a reader but you missed some of the children's classics, I encourage you to make a U-turn and go back for them. *Little Women, Pilgrim's Progress, Anne of Green Gables, Robinson Crusoe, Black Beauty, Treasure Island, Alice's Adventures in Wonderland, Heidi, Moby Dick, Winnie the Pooh,* and the Chronicles of Narnia occur to me as fun places to explore children's books. These are a great way to jump-start your brain and refresh your reading skills, besides being great reads.

After, say, six months in children's classics, I predict you will be hooked on reading. It gets in your brain, imagination, and, best of all, your heart.

I like to read a classic and a current release at the same time. Going back and forth between the two keeps me mentally alert. I confess, though, that I can't do it if there are too many characters. Then I'll have Marilla (of the Anne of Green Gables series) cooking crepes in Julia Child's kitchen.

Oh, did I mention I'm a cookbook fanatic? Not to be confused with someone who actually turns on a stove or flips a flapjack.

I have cookbooks and food magazines galore. I am a Pioneer-Woman-Ree-Drummond fan. Big-time. I love her approach, humor, and recipes, which I actually use. And may I say, she makes me look good. Her rolls, potatoes, onion strings, and pineapple upside-down cake are amazing. (Tip: When transferring cake from cast iron pan onto cake dish, do so gingerly. Otherwise, the weight of the iron skillet striking against the glass cake stand could cause it to shatter and your cake to break into enough crumbs that you could help Jesus feed the multitudes on the hillside. Don't ask me how I know this.)

I'm also a Susan Branch follower. She hand designs and paints every page of her cookbooks with a family whimsy that's charming. Several of her recipes have become traditions in my home. Susan's Scotch Eggs make a perfect holiday breakfast; her French toast garners enthusiastic applause; and her baked apples filled with oatmeal, walnuts, and brown sugar are perfect for a chilly night next to a stoked fire. Her books are readily available online but harder these days to find in-store. My favorite is probably *Christmas: The Heart of the Home* although I also love her *Vineyard Seasons* and find her *Summer Book* just plain refreshing. Okay, I confess: I have everything she's written and reference them all.

I recently have added to my collection the Barefoot Contessa's cookbooks. Her directions and recipes are friendly and classy. Not an easy combination. I love her account of her first trip to Paris. It's romantic and intriguing. I love her approach to stocking her kitchen because she keeps it simple. I tend to be a gadget junkie; so it's good to have someone remind me I don't need a whatchamacallit that carves wavy grooves into a lemon rind.

I have to say, the Lord has taken me through some emotionally turbulent seasons in the kitchen. The creative process and the end results are healing to all the unfinished business inside of me. I can't explain it, but I've experienced it many times. The longer I sift, whisk, and puree, the more blended and less lumpy

I personally feel. Maybe it serves as a distraction that helps pull me out of my slumps. For whatever reason, cooking is its own kind of therapy, and cookbooks make good mood manuals for rainy hearts. One season I made so many pies to expend my anxiety that we couldn't find enough people to give them to. I mean, who wants a pie full of angst?

Speaking of recipes, here's my simple syrup for reading:

1. I confess I don't finish every book I start. There. I said it aloud. Sometimes they don't turn out to be what I thought they would. Other times I lose interest. But, quite honestly, according to stats, I don't have that many reading years left. So I've given myself permission to move on. If after thirty to forty pages, the book hasn't caught my attention, I pull back. I admit I possibly miss some great reads by not hanging in there, but unless I hear from a dedicated reader that a book starts slow and then picks up speed, I'm off to the mall to buy fuzzy slippers.

2. I also have given myself (hold on to your socks) permission to write in my books. Yes, I'm a book scribbler in the highest sense. For some that's not an option or preference, but it helps me to think and to recover thoughts later if I've marked them or commented on a line. I find my written interaction helps to connect me more deeply to the content. So I read with a pen in hand. Many people date their reads, which I think is smart, especially

if the book is one you will circle back to again and again. Others rate their books with a code. My rating system is simple: if I love the book, I keep it; if I don't, I give it away to someone I think might appreciate the topic and style. Ta-da!

3. I try to keep my reading topics diverse: fiction, non-fiction, history, wisdom literature, art, biographies, cookbooks. A wide girth of material keeps our interaction with others lively and protects friends from enduring lopsided conversations on our "obsession." (I know a fellow who reads only railroad books and magazines. I can only go around that track so many times before I get plumb dizzy. *Woo! Woo!*)

That's it. Told you it was simple. If a book isn't working for you, move on. If you can bear it, fully own your books by writing notes in the margins (at least try it). And keep your reading topics diverse.

The hardest part of becoming a reader is beginning. I know. I have to sometimes chat myself into a book: "Stop bebopping all over God's green acre, Patsy. Pin your britches to yonder chair and focus."

Focus is a diminishing attribute in our electronic world of fast-flickering games and abbreviated text. It's hard to read a book or have a lingering conversation while we thumb-scroll through our texts, blow up pigs (a game), and scan rooms for new faces to tweet about. It's not just that the studious art of reading and meaningful conversation is disappearing, but the courtesy of our undivided attention has been replaced with a few disconnected glances. Besides sending the wrong message to people we truly care about, all this eye flitting and mind scampering is robbing us of the gift of focus.

If I discover a book that I love, one that wraps itself around me and whispers and shouts in ways I can receive, then I become the town crier. Just ask my friends. I can't tell enough people about books that bless me. I become a walking book review.

That happened recently with author Ian Cron's book *Chasing Francis*. I was smitten by his writing style and the fine weave of the story. Ian is a sentence crafter, squeezing elixir from every word. The story surrounds a minister who, in a crisis of faith, ends up in Italy on an unexpected quest tracing the life of Saint Francis of Assisi. The book is a combination of fiction and nonfiction that comes with a built-in study guide.

Les is what one might call a nonreader. Oh, he likes the sports section of the newspaper, a good map, and calorie-laden, large-print menus, but that's about it. To my delight, when he casually picked up *Chasing Francis* from the coffee table so he would have a place to set down his cup, he didn't let the book go. He read every single page of it and loved it. Any book that could inspire that is worth checking out. That's all I'm saying.

Another 2010 book that caught me by surprise was David Teems's *Majestie*, a biography of King James. That genre typically is not on my radar—until I opened Teems's book and read the first pages. I confess, my knee-jerk reaction was "I'm not smart enough to read this." The word choices were formidable, but once I relaxed with the intelligence of this offering, I think I grew new brain cells. David's ability to use language, humor, and history kept me riveted page after revealing page.

In early 2010, author, artist, dear friend, and dedicated reader Randy Elrod introduced me to two reads that filled my bucket. They are the types of books I return to again and again. One is on the life of Leonardo da Vinci; the other is a hefty volume on books, *The Joy of Reading: A Passionate Guide to 189 of the World's Best Authors and Their Works*, by Charles Van Doren.

The Joy of Reading has stayed at my bedside for a year and will continue to reside there. It makes for great reading at my fingertips during those last moments before I fade into the pillow. I have read, reread, and referenced it repeatedly. Van Doren's reviews are some of the best I've encountered. He begins with Homer's *The Iliad* and *The Odyssey*, written approximately twenty-seven hundred years ago, and takes us through to J. K. Rowling. That's a lot of reading acreage. Van Doren even outlines a ten-year reading program to help us journey through all these amazing books. While I don't plan to read all of them, I love having their essence instilled in my brain.

My brain leaks, which is why I keep reviewing this literary time capsule, hoping more will stick in the crevices. Van Doren includes a biographical essence on each author, which I found eye-opening and inspiring. I loved reading whom each writer was friends with, like Edith Wharton and Henry James, and how they influenced each other's work. Van Doren gives a historical sense of the timetable in which each book was penned and how it was received by the public and critics. Then he reviews the work without spoiling the pudding. He will definitely whet your appetite to make a trip to the local bookstore and leave with an armload of word-rich entertainment at its best. It's as if he wanted to give us the best viewing window in the house.

I think we should now and again read books that rattle our comfort zones, that challenge our belief systems, that present fresh thoughts on old topics. In other words, books that make us think. It's easy to get stodgy and miserably comfortable. If you're easily offended and defensive regarding what you believe, you might want to shore it up with a doctrinal study so you feel steadier on your faith feet. I'm a huge proponent of reading materials that nurture our souls, refresh our perspectives, and support our belief systems as well.

I've been a Max Lucado fan for years, but recently I've especially needed his gentle pen. When life's winds blow fiercely, I search out writers who kindly invite me to sit by the warm embers of their experience. Ken Gire has that kind of invitational pen as well. I'm rereading his *Windows of the Soul*, allowing the fresh breeze of his insights to remind me I'm not alone in my wonderings and wanderings. His contemplative approach is the contrast I need to my chaotic pace; it brings some balance.

That's one of the wonderful things about a book: it companions you—at least for twelve chapters' worth. In the movie *Shadowland*, about C. S. Lewis's love story, a line spoke to me: "We read to know we are not alone."

Some books settle down within us and become reference points throughout our lives. Who do you quote? Shakespeare? Churchill? Jane Austen? How good of God to use words—his and others'—to inspire, instruct, and encourage us.

Reading has profoundly changed my story. God has used the stories of others to help fuse together my fractured life. In the privacy and safety of my reading chair, I could consider the way God worked in someone else's life, which opened my heart to a more expansive work being done within me. Following someone else's journey can help us to be braver, more creative, more forgiving, and more loving.

Need a higher perspective? Reach for a book . . . one full of the dynamics of living life as an adventure.

The Art Gallery

Artists: *Randy Elrod*. The picture that hangs in our living room is a favorite of both my husband's and mine. It is the original and was a gift from the artist to Les for his birthday. It's called the *Time Traveler*. An old man is reading a newspaper. Simple yet profound. The sun is warming the man's forehead and beard, giving him an enlightened countenance. He appears hearty, strong, wise, determined, and informed. Everyone who enters our home comments on it. You can view it online at my website: www.patsyclairmont.com.

Carl Spitzweg (again). Here's what's funny: I thought I'd never seen any of Spitzweg's work, but it turns out I have a print of his, which delights me, hanging in my dining room, called *The Bookworm*. Who knew?

A servant in a wealthy home is on a ladder in front of a wall of books in the library. He appears to be returning copies to their rightful places, probably some his employer had left out the evening prior. But the servant has opened a volume and now can't tear himself away. Besides the book he's reading, he has another one open in his other hand, one large tome tucked under his arm, and one between his knees. That's my kind of studious guy. Dangling from his back pocket is a cleaning cloth, suggesting he was going to dust while he was up there. Many a time a good housecleaning intention has been lost to a great book. I call that prioritizing.

Unknown artist. Over our fireplace is a print on canvas of a young couple who are seated and leaning over a slanted board desk. The young man has a pencil, and he's writing something while the young woman is watching with loving interest. I'm almost certain that he's writing a book and seeking her input on his outline. At least that's what I tell myself. They could be drawing a house plan or thinking through a business strategy. I don't know the name of the print or the artist. I continue to keep my eyes open in my research, hoping to find it. I love the visual story going on between them. They are leaning in, heads touching, eyes on the desk, and his hand tenderly shelters hers. It suggests they are on the same page, dreaming together, and feel safe in each other's company.

Winslow Homer. I'm a fan of American painter Winslow

Homer. In fact, it has been my goal to see as many of his works during my lifetime as I can. Homer did at least four well-known paintings of women perusing books: *Woman Reading Under an Oak*, *Woman Reading on a Stone Porch*, *Sunlight and Shadows* (a woman reading in a hammock), and *A New Novel*. The last is my personal favorite.

I've wondered why so many paintings during that era show women reading. So I did a little research. I learned that women involved in such a risqué indulgence, especially reading novels, were considered almost scandalous. Winslow Homer either was enjoying the scandal, or he was helping to condition society to a new standard that included the acceptance of women being allowed to make their own reading choices. We've come a long way. Whew!

Music: *Symphonic Praise and Worship* CDs, including the Amade String Orchestra (gloriously gentle).

Scripture: "Then those who feared the LORD spoke to one another, and the LORD listened and heard them; so a book of remembrance was written before Him for those who fear the LORD and who meditate on His name." (Malachi 3:16 NKJV)

Chapter 9

Stained Glass Puzzles

L ife is puzzling. God is mysterious. People are odd.

I admit I am Queen of Peculiar, and I married His Highness King Strangeness. We're layered in outlandishness and selfishness. I do believe we have the makings of a hit reality series or a *New York Times* bestseller.

Am I the only one who's perplexed a good deal of the time? Hello. I hear myself say, "Why did he do that?" "What was she thinking?" "You have to be kidding!" Head scratching has become a habit as I try to figure out folks.

I guess that's why I own so many books on personality types, relationship strategies, and how to improve communications. But, honestly, some people don't seem to fit the printed profiles. They are . . . puzzling.

But it's not just people that send me circling my brain for answers; it's circumstances as well. Last summer we officially moved from Michigan to Tennessee. That was huge. We thought we wouldn't be impossibly far from our children; yet we would be in a more moderate weather zone and in an area already chock-full of friends. The choice has been great . . . but so far you can erase moderate weather.

Since we first arrived last winter, the area had its coldest temperatures in years; spring arrived, and with it came the one-hundred-year flood, which sent us scampering for higher ground as the Harpeth River surged up our driveway and lapped at our front porch while filling our cellar and drowning our hot water heater. I knew we were in trouble when the National Guard arrived at our door, wanting to carry us to safety. Spring was quickly followed by summer, with the most consecutive days over ninety degrees in recorded Tennessee history, leaving angry blisters on our lawn furniture. That was topped off with the coolest, most colorless fall Tennesseans can recount. We are now in the snowiest winter they can recall. (I'm beginning to wonder if their recaller is just plumb broke.)

> It is one of man's curious idiosyncrasies to create difficulties for the pleasure of resolving them.
>
> —JOSEPH DE MAISTRE

So what's with that? Where's the way it usually is? Where's the expected? Where's normal?

Years ago I wrote a book titled *Normal Is Just a Setting on Your Dryer*, yet even knowing that "normal" is a myth, I still swag my head when it doesn't materialize. Life, people, and circumstances are not—I repeat, not—predictable. Nor is moving.

I know moving. We are intimately acquainted. I've been slinging boxes and crates in cars and trucks for as long as I can remember. So I anticipated that this move, number forty-something, would be a cinch, not taking into consideration that once again I had ridiculous expectations for the predictable.

We were in Tennessee, and we had just signed closing papers, when my husband announced he had booked me on a flight to Michigan so I could pack up our belongings and bring them to our new home. Huh? Me? By myself? That's not the way my moving script read. I thought to myself, *You've got to be kidding.* But when I pondered the arrangement, I knew that was the best way to do it. My husband has growing disabilities that prevent him from standing steady on his feet and keep him from walking well. Besides, we have different opinions on what constitutes a treasure, and ever since he tossed out my wedding dress thirteen moves ago, I tend to oversuperintend on moving day.

So off I went, knowing that our two sons would assist me. Except when I arrived, our youngest son and his family had just left on a ten-day vacation in California, and our eldest was sick in bed. Hmm. Well, that left little ol' me. I glanced around and thought, *Be a big girl and get to packing, honey.*

That was when it happened. Queen of Peculiar, for some reason known not even to me, decided to start her packing efforts with a clock perched on a high—I said *high*—shelf. I scampered onto a chair, then balanced myself on the chair's back and stepped up from there onto a marble shelf. From there I was able to pull down the clock. *Down* being the operative word. Somehow, going down was so much more rapid than the ascent had been. Rapid but not graceful—not even a little—as my foot missed the back of the chair, and I catapulted backward toward the floor. Partway down my fall was interrupted by the marble hearth, as my hip slammed against it, and then I was tossed onto the floor, rag doll–style.

Sprawled, staring up at the ceiling, I thought, *Did I forget to say my prayers this morning?* Isn't it human nature to think that if only I had said the right Bible verse upon arising and perhaps said grace aloud before I ate that Krispy Kreme, maybe I wouldn't have fallen? I then decided this was a good time to have devotions since I was afraid to move and find out the hip bone was no longer connected to the backbone. That's when I realized my phone was in the kitchen, no one was expected to come by the house until the following evening, and the doors to the house were all locked. Uh-oh.

Some time passed, maybe twenty minutes, before I gently tested my parts. Eventually I pulled myself up onto my feet and slowly moved around. Nothing was broken. Well, the clock may never strike twelve again, but I was intact. I remained sore for a few weeks, and I sported the worst set of bruises in my life, but I was able to carry on with the job at hand. No more climbing, though, and I groaned a lot when I did certain activities . . . like move or breathe.

We had more old belongings than we had new house space because we had sized down. So deciding what to take, pack, give away, and sell was difficult, making this move unlike any we had been through. This wasn't the norm. I was used to going from small to a tiny bit larger, but this was the reverse, and I had—how shall I say?—accumulated a wad of stuff. It happens. And during forty-eight years, one can hang on to more than she realizes.

We hired friends to pack the truck and drive it to Tennessee. By the time the truck was crammed full, our two brave workers, Dan and Randy, were bone tired. We knew we needed fresh recruits at the new residence to help unload, which we didn't think was an issue because we have a circle of friends in our neighborhood we call "the campus." Guess what? They were all out of town on preplanned trips, most for business. Five men had offered their muscles; all five were gone. Who could have predicted that? Now what? I was flummoxed.

Our Michigan friends showed up with the truck, look-ing road weary after a ten-hour haul. I hated to tell them that "Bruiser," my new nickname, might be their only helper. But then two strangers came to my door and announced they had come to help. I stood dumbstruck. They were like angels, wings fluttering, announcing a miracle was about to take place. Finding my voice, I asked, "Who are you, and how did you know we needed your help?" One man smiled and said, "The church Twitter."

I looked out the door, and cars were pulling up all down our street. By the time the folks got out of their vehicles, they numbered twenty-five workers. Actually, I could have held a concert and charged admission right then and there because among the good souls who were helping were Nicole C. Mullen;

her husband, David Mullen, a singer in his own right; the NCM team of teen singers; Mandisa; Chance Scoggins, the one who posted the church Twitter; and Kara Tualatai. Oh, yes, and author-speaker Lisa Harper was there. I'm convinced after watching her single-handedly lift boxes the size of the Grand Ole Opry that she could have unloaded the truck by herself, given the gospel, and taken up a collection.

This was definitely not the norm. It was a you-have-to-be-kidding moment of the sweetest kind. What would have taken us at best two and a half days, plus years of therapy, took two and a half hours and doughnuts from the deli.

Why would I want to predict God when he is so mercifully unpredictable and far more creative than anything I could come up with?

"It is of the LORD's mercies that we are not consumed, because his compassions fail not. They are new every morning: great is thy faithfulness" (Lamentations 3:22–23 KJV).

We've now been in our home for six months. It's friendly yet at times puzzling. I find it takes experience to learn a living rhythm in a new place. First off, it was discordant trying to remember where I put things. I ran a marathon, jogging from cupboard to closet in search of my important stuff (glasses, underwear, toenail clippers . . . just keeping it real). And nothing in this house—nothing—is positioned the same as in our last house. So I'm constantly flailing about, looking for light switches, doors, and locks. Somebody keeps moving them. When I finally find one, I think, *What was he thinking?*

Whoever *he* is. I mean, we have a couple of light switch plates that are about the height of a gnat's knee while others are level with my eyebrows when they are arched high with surprise. With these transitional days, trust me: I'm constantly bewildered.

With Christmas came the job of figuring out where the tree should go, how to decorate the porch, and where to hide presents. I did a great job on the latter because we still haven't found where I stashed some of them.

Our kitchen has a couple of features I've never lived with before. One is a Dutch door, the kind Mr. Ed sticks his head through. To know Mr. Ed you have to either watch Nick at Night or be exceedingly old. Ed was a talking palomino full of opinions. I don't have a palomino, but I do have opinions, many of them about my stove.

In addition to the Dutch door, the stove is the other odd feature in my kitchen, and it's called an Aga, which is a Swedish company. It took us two days to figure out the reason the burners wouldn't light was because the gas company had turned off the gas. Then, in the middle of preparing dinner for guests, the electric stove unit went out, and we had to bring in an electrician to add another line. When I tried to fix biscuits, I learned that Europeans use a smaller cookie sheet. No matter which way I tried to slide it in, it wasn't going to fit. Also, the stove isn't as deep as American stoves, so many of my larger pots and pans were too wide and long. Add to that the broiler only functions when the door is fully open, and the oven requires two different knobs adjusted for it to even turn on. I was mystified by the design of this contraption most of the time.

One day I pulled a chair up to the stove, took out the book of directions (told you I love books), and stared and stared, while scratching my head. That's when it hit me . . . someone had put the knobs back on the unit in the wrong order, which explained why a thirty-minute baking time took an hour and a half. I thought I was baking, but I actually was defrosting.

The stove and I are now tight. We have worked out most of our issues with each other, and I now find her winsome. We purchased a few new cooking utensils, the size Ken and Barbie use in their dollhouse, and voilà, dinner is served. Word to the wise: you may want to bring supplementary takeout.

All that to say, we are always going to rub up against life's confusing parts. Nothing is static. What once was, may no longer be. Try as we might to nail things down, to keep them in place, they have a way of morphing into something else—whether it's changing weather patterns, adjusting to a different location, or everyday activities that frustrate and challenge us.

But I personally think one of the most disconcerting is people. Try as I might to carefully catalog people, they won't stay on their pages.

Two weeks after our son Marty was released from the hospital, Les needed to go to the doctor to pick up prescriptions. Marty rode along with his dad to have a reprieve from cabin fever during his long journey toward healing. A short time later Les called to tell me that the doctor wanted him to have some tests.

"I'll want to be with you when you have those," I mentioned. And we hung up.

Marty called back in a few minutes to report that he had just talked with the doctor.

Confused as to why he would be talking with the doctor, I asked, "Why? Aren't you feeling well?"

"I'm fine," he assured me. "It's Dad. Didn't he tell you what's going on?"

Evidently not.

It turned out the medical staff thought Les was having a heart attack, and they were sending him by ambulance (while he was talking to me) to the same hospital Marty had just been released from. When Les dialed me, they were putting him on the gurney—a small detail he forgot to mention. Les ended up having a stent put in, and he was home after a few days.

> Man is born broken. He lives mending. The grace of God is glue.
>
> —Eugene O'Neill

Where was his mind when he forgot to mention the life-threatening detail that he might be having a coronary and was that very moment being rushed to the hospital? He's had three heart attacks; so maybe he thought it was old news. Talk about puzzling.

If people aren't enough to confound me, then there's God, who refuses to be defined by our upbringing, churches, doctrines, opinions, or even well-written books. No matter how carefully and tightly we stitch our belief system together, God keeps editing and enlarging our concept of him through our experiences, prayers, and the world we live in. We try to make excuses for his seeming lack of involvement in certain crucial matters, not so much to protect his reputation as to protect our belief system.

Here's why I think that is. If our whip-stitched doctrines turn out to be inaccurate, it threatens to unravel us. Is it possible we have more confidence in our doctrines than we do in our Deliverer? Just asking.

I've come to realize that what I was taught early on wasn't all true. Much was; some wasn't. No one meant to mislead me. They, too, thought that if they could explain God on paper, it would keep them safe. Now I'm in my last season on Earth, and I feel like, in some ways, a babe in my faith. For as much as I think I know, there's even more that I'm not sure of. I guess I shouldn't be surprised that God is cloaked in mystery because he is pure spirit. I'm not. He is absolute in his holiness. I'm not. He is blameless. I'm not (except in Christ). He is love. I'm ornery by nature. He is mysterious. I'm a complicated puzzle to myself and to those who know me, but to God I'm an easy read, an open book, a known story.

> Preach the gospel at all times—if necessary, use words.
>
> —SAINT FRANCIS OF ASSISI

The puzzling pieces of our lives, like the misshapen glass pieces in a stained glass masterpiece, don't seem to fit until the

Creator sands, foils, and solders them into place. Then we see, and what looked hopelessly missing is pieced together in such a way that the picture appears seamless.

I'm committed by faith to Christ, in whom I believe, but I ponder with uncertainty many of the particulars. Mrs. She-Who-Thinks-She-Has-the-Answers has learned instead to take shelter under the marvel of his mystery. For there I don't have to know answers; I'm just asked to trust. God doesn't ask me to defend his reputation or to debate with others doctrinally, but he does make it clear I'm to love.

We are temporarily confined to this planet in a leaky earth suit. One day that will change, and then we will see what we can't imagine, and we will understand what we can't comprehend. Then, and only then, the puzzling aspects will be solved, the last pieces will slide into place.

The Art Gallery

Painting: *The Three Musicians*. Check this out on Google and Wikipedia.

One of the most puzzling artists to me is the Spanish painter Pablo Picasso. I can grasp some of his work but not a lot of it without help. Generally speaking, he was a cubist and a pointillist. One thing for sure, he was prolific and versatile. Pablo constantly was morphing in his work, depending on where he was living, who he was socializing with, and what was happening in the world around him. He lived a sordid and sad life overall, even though he achieved fame and financial wealth.

"Give me a museum, and I'll fill it," Pablo is often quoted as having said. "My mother said to me, 'If you are a soldier, you will become a general. If you are a monk, you will become the Pope.' Instead, I was a painter and became Picasso."

Puzzle: The Guinness record holder for the largest commercial puzzle, "Life: The Greatest Challenge," was designed by artist Royce B. McClure. It's more than fourteen feet long and five feet wide and has twenty-four thousand pieces. Get this: it weighs, in-box, twenty-six pounds. "Honey, would you help me get the puzzle out?" Talk about a project that will keep the kids busy. Ha. Trust me, that's no kiddie task. You really should look at it, it's quite beautiful (Google "world's largest puzzle"). It's full of aquatic life, sailboats, birds, hot-air balloons, and wildlife. A three-minute video gives you detailed views of this masterpiece.

Here's my quandary. Where does one assemble it? A gymnasium? The Astrodome? It comes packaged in four sections.

Music: "When Life Gets Broken," Sandi Patty

Scripture: "This is the plan devised against the whole earth; and this is the hand that is stretched out against all the nations. For the LORD of hosts has planned, and who can frustrate it? And as for His stretched-out hand, who can turn it back?" (Isaiah 14:26–27)

The lot is cast into the lap,
But its every decision is from the LORD.

(PROVERBS 16:33)

Just as He chose us in Him before the foundation of the world, that
we would be holy and blameless before Him.

(EPHESIANS 1:4)

Chapter 10

Stained Glass Nature

Come on in; the weather's, uh, it's, well, changeable. Like life. Yep, like a stained glass puzzle. Thunderous one day and lavender sweet the next.

Have you ever wondered what the weather was like during creation? I think odd thoughts like that. I know by the time the Lord God was done that it was good, but while it was going on, what kind of atmospheric turbulence occurred? I mean, there must have been quite a clamor when he was filling the storehouses with hail and lightning; arranging the stars by name ("Harold, I said to the left . . . No, your other left"); setting boundaries on the ocean ("I said 'stay,' and I mean it"); corralling light; setting torch to the comets; and spinning Hula-Hoops around Saturn.

In prior chapters we've chatted about music, poetry, prayer, books, puzzles, and more—all windows that have brought healing and color to my stained glass heart and probably to yours. It's our human way to search out relief when we hurt, and it's God's way to provide comfort and insight.

One window we haven't peeked through in these pages is

nature (other than listening to the birds sing). God's handiwork declares him day after day, and the declarations become our education, our inspiration, and our restoration. When we have ears to hear and eyes to see, we're left breathless by his visual power displayed throughout the universe, and we're silenced when we detect his whispers in a meandering brook. That a holy God would speak through river pebbles to my stony heart is humbling.

> I love to think of nature as an unlimited broadcasting station, through which God speaks to us every hour, if we will only tune in.
>
> —George Washington Carver

People travel the world over to applaud creation's art and to stand amazed when they visit Victoria Falls, the Grand Canyon, Mount Everest, Niagara Falls, Antarctica, and the ocean's edge. Just think. All that and more was wrought from God's creative hand with us in mind. Why would he purposely color the world with splendor?

I was reminded afresh of God's presence in nature this past week, as I once again took refuge in our friend's hilltop cabin, Round Cove. I love its wild comforts and serene storms. I feel safe and cared for there. Somehow it gives me permission to come home to myself. My daily lifestyle is one of travel and busyness, but when I step into Round Cove, my fervor dissipates. Before long I have cozied into a corner to gaze, read, and nap. Ah.

When we first arrived at Round Cove, the cloud-laden skies,

purple with intensity, howled at the cabin windows. Winds snapped branches, felled trees, and hailed on the tin roof. A cacophony of nature, a concert of wonder, filled with songs of glory that you could hear if you leaned into the music.

Swirls of dry leaves were lifted higher than treetops and then rained down on the cove below, anointing the woods with its life . . . the repurposing of the land. How inspiring to see withered leaves in flight. Dead on the branch one moment, then alive in the storm. Fly, leaf, fly. Ride the winds.

Near the barn, winged cornstalks were aflutter with blackbirds. Next to my window, a feathered ruby perched deep on a frenzied branch. Between tree trunks a summer hammock ballooned with worry, its ropes taunt from hugging the trees.

By evening you could sense the storm's final word was near. The woods hushed for a moment, as if listening for footsteps. Suddenly the cabin's tin roof shook as chilling winds unleashed again, this time companioned with snow. The flakes rolled through the woods

> Everybody needs beauty as well as bread, places to play in and pray in, where nature may heal and give strength to body and soul.
>
> —JOHN MUIR

like swarms of glass fireflies searching for refuge. Finally, near daybreak, they huddled in mounds below my window.

By full morning light, fog had hushed the storm's fury to a whisper. The trees rested from head wagging and now stood straight, silhouetted against the rising mist. With arms raised, the trees appeared to be worshipping. Birds dangled from twigs, noted gemstones that then darted across the snow. Their erratic flight turned to cursive script that left fading messages in the crisp air.

Yes, creation causes us to stand and celebrate. Not to worship creation, which we willingly applaud, but to worship the Creator—he who was before the sun, moon, and stars.

> God writes the gospel not in the Bible alone, but on trees and flowers and clouds and stars.
>
> —MARTIN LUTHER

I couldn't just sit and look at the snow through the window the morning after the storm. I needed to be out in it. Since I hadn't brought boots, I borrowed a pair three sizes too big that came up above my knees; I wore two pairs of socks, slipped into a pair of men's hunting pants, cinched them up under my arms with my husband's belt, tied the belt in a knot around me, then added my sweater, vest, coat, mittens, and a camouflage stocking cap. Got the picture? Let's just say that when I walked out the door, it was probably a coincidence, but the rooster screamed. Then I thought I heard snickering from a clump of nearby trees.

My excursion lasted three minutes and forty-two seconds, which is when I fell cell phone first, followed quickly by my face, into a stony snowbank. I pulled myself up, did a little snow removal to find my anatomy, and discovered that every time I breathed, my glasses fogged over and crystallized. I waddled and tripped my way back to the cabin, all thirty feet, and began the unveiling process. Eleven layers lighter, I reentered the cabin, perched myself on a chair, and watched with utter delight as the sun skittered across frosty branches. Ah, perspective.

For some reason, my snowy journey reminded me of an antique picture I once owned. The painting was left behind in one of our house moves, and by the time I realized I didn't have it anymore, the home had been occupied a couple of times, and the picture was gone. The painting was of an old woman walking on a wooded path in the dead of winter. On her shoulders she carried a bundle of twigs, her head covered in a scarf. She wore a long, brown wool coat and short boots. In the distance the sun was setting, spilling warm ochre across the horizon and the remnants of day. Between the woman and the sunset was a cabin with amber lamp lights in the windows and smoke rising from the chimney. An ice-covered pond in front of the small dwelling chilled the landscape even more.

When I first saw this painting, I just knew the woman was almost home. I found that so comforting. For then she could lay down the weight carried on her back and melt the chill from her bones. I

> Nature is full of genius, full of the divinity; so that not a snowflake escapes its fashioning hand.
>
> —HENRY DAVID THOREAU

could imagine her soaking her weary feet in a basin of water and sipping a cup of soup, glad for the warmth on her stiff hands. And I wanted to believe she had fresh bread, aged cheese, and smoked fish in the knapsack that hung on her back under the kindling and that someone she loved who was kind to her was waiting to share in the bounty. Perhaps it was her dear husband, who could no longer bear the trek to town, but who could still stir the embers and light the lamps.

The cabin represented such hope, with its warm presence in the midst of the cold scene. (If you have my picture, please return it. I miss it.)

> The world is mud-luscious and puddle-wonderful.
>
> —E. E. CUMMINGS

Winter represents so many things to people, often depending on one's age. For some, winter is sleds, skis, and hot cocoa. For others, possibly the old woman on the path, it's hardship and drudgery. And for others yet, it represents their last season on Earth.

Two years ago my friend Carol left for heaven in a winter snowfall, the most beautiful snowscape I had ever seen. The kind where the world turns into a fairy tale as the snow sculptures beauty out of everything it touches. Carol was an artist who did likewise. She was a mud-licious, puddle-wonderful kind of girl—wide-eyed with childlike delight and her heart happy with infectious joy. Carol's laughter and tears, always near, often anointed her friends as we gathered around her hearth. She loved Jesus, and the deep ache in her heart was to see that all those whom she loved would love him too.

With Carol's death, we who cherished her felt the bitter chill of loss and winter's grip on our bones. But we don't grieve as some without hope, for we understand that the brutality of death and these years without her are but for a season. Spring will come. Carol saw that in a vision God gave her before she died. She was running across a field full of flowers with her disabled grandson, Randy. Carol didn't know it then, but Randy would join his grandma in heaven five weeks after her death. Winter has left them both. Their forever is springtime.

I will never stop aching for her . . . here. Sometimes I want to say to Jesus, "You have my Carol. Could you please return her? I miss her." And then I remember the field of flowers.

Vincent van Gogh painted a canvas called *Field of Flowers*. I wasn't familiar with the painting until recently, and as I studied it, I was confused. The fields were swaths of different colored flowers planted by peasants with carefully executed paths between the sections.

That's not what troubled me. It was the trees in the distance. They were barren. Not a leaf or suspected bud. How could all those flowers be in full bloom yet the trees be fruitless? A man walks in the midst of the blossom plots and seems by his body language to be detached from the beauty he's in. He appears to be looking in the distance, perhaps at the stark trees, rather than delighting in the immediate splendor.

I wonder if this canvas is more about the painter than the place? Van Gogh had just made a physical change in his life, having left a failed relationship; so perhaps he feels more an observer of than a participant in his surroundings, and that sense of detachment came out in his work. His life was marked by storms of anxiety, which led to mental illness.

Maybe the trees represent the peasant's hard life. Or maybe the artist wanted all the focus on the flowers.

Van Gogh served as an assistant Methodist minister for several years when he was young, as he struggled with how to tell others the gospel and paint. He, in the words of many, was a difficult man, and he was relatively unknown as an artist during his lifetime. Historians say van Gogh was a tortured soul and often ill. He suffered many losses throughout his life, perpetuating his melancholy. He drank too much, smoked obsessively, slept too little, and seldom ate. He created many self-portraits, which makes me wonder if Vincent was trying to *fix* what he didn't like, to produce a better version of himself. Almost all of his paintings were done in the last two years of his life and were brilliant. He died by his own hand at the age of thirty-seven. He ended up using the hand that had been given to him to create beauty to bring about tragedy.

Today Vincent van Gogh is considered one of history's greatest painters.

His life reminds me of my tendency to miss or to overlook the beauty of the moment for the uncertainty of what's ahead. If ever there was a story to nudge us to stop and smell the flowers, it is van Gogh's. When he wasn't fighting a battle with his humanity, which he never came to terms with, he was producing the work of a genius. What a picture of how potentially gifted we are—and yet how fractured.

God won't make us behave. I personally believe the truths we've been given through the Holy Spirit (Scripture, prayer, nature) help lead us to the integration of our broken parts toward wholeness and sanity. The more we choose to stray, the more we tend to fray. Legitimate mental disorders exist, and I'm not talking about those. I'm speaking of the demise of my own life mentally, emotionally, and relationally as I made a succession of poor choices, indulged my weaknesses, fanned my sadness, and separated myself from others.

How's your self-portrait? How do you see yourself? How do you talk to you?

Quite honestly, I still have to be reminded by others to talk nice to myself. I forget. I'm not always kind in my inner messages. When those comments start to leak out and someone brings them to my attention, I know it's time to "have a little talk with Jesus" . . . again. We can't fix ourselves—that's the transforming work of Christ—but he allows us to be active participants in our get-well program.

Van Gogh did poorly in relationships. Not with a few people but with everyone except his brother. If you or someone you love can't deal with people without anger and constant feelings of rejection, it's time to obtain help. I did.

We were meant to relate with others. And while relationships can be tricky weather to navigate, they are meant to help us grow, love more purely, and have healthy connection, which initially can feel odd and intimidating if we haven't experienced it before. Making changes from childishness to adult behavior can be awkward and at first can feel like shame instead of gain. But that feeling is called *vulnerability*. Press on. Those feelings are important to intimacy (human closeness), and they help us to move toward a life-giving perspective.

What do relationships have to do with nature? Think about phrases we use to describe our connections with others: She was a fair-weather friend. They had a stormy relationship. He rained on my parade. She was my honeysuckle rose. His response was icy. She thundered her disapproval. He was the apple of my eye. She was a breath of fresh air. He had a sunny disposition. I guess, when we couldn't think of terms big enough to describe others, we threw open a window and borrowed from the grand outdoors.

Speaking of a sunny disposition, if I ever want to brighten my day, I head for my screened-in back porch. I get sun but not too much. I get a bug or two but not too many. I can see the trees, birds, flowers, and I can hear the church bells wafting my favorite old hymns through the maple's branches. Right now winter is blustering about; so I have to wait a couple of months before I toddle out in my capris, sink into a rocking chair, and allow the warm breezes to trace my face and ruffle my hair. I remember as a kid that I loved to run barefoot in the cool grass. Not so much anymore. But I never tire of the restoration to my mind and soul that comes with a good dose of nature.

Take two swigs and call me in the morning.

Earth's crammed with heaven,
And every common bush afire with God.

(ELIZABETH BARRETT BROWNING)

The Art Gallery

Music: *The Four Seasons*, Vivaldi; "How Great Thou Art," Sandi Patty; "River God," Nichole Nordeman.

Video: YouTube of John Muir's life (naturalist, conservationist), parts 1 and 2. Both parts are short. One day Muir went for a walk in the woods and didn't come out for fifteen years. He covered one thousand miles on foot. Now, there was a man you couldn't let out very often. Just sayin'.

Museum: *Detroit Institute of Art*. *The White Veil* by Willard Metcalf; *The Four Leaf Clover* by Winslow Homer.

I spent weeks one summer as a twelve-year-old staying with relatives in Kentucky. My favorite activity was searching for four-leaf clovers; so Homer's oil painting of this young girl, holding her prize, stirs sweet memories. I love the way he captures the viewer's attention with shocks of color in this verdant setting.

Scripture:

> *The earth is the Lord's, and everything in it.*
>
> (Psalm 24:1 NIV)

> *As the deer pants for the water brooks,*
> *So my soul pants for You, O God.*
>
> (Psalm 42:1)

> *Great and marvellous are thy works.*
>
> (Revelation 15:3 KJV)

Chapter 11

Stained Glass Profusion, a Garden

When I go to the grocery store, I always enter through the same door because just inside is an array of blossoms that delights my eyes, nose, and soul. Bouquets of lilies, roses, and daisies, to name a few, crowd around clay pots of daffodils and hyacinths proclaiming, "Spring is near!" Never mind your fur-lined jacket; just take a gander at those pink tulips, and I promise yellow butterflies will flit through your chilly mind, warming your thoughts. The blossoming colors make me want to do a happy dance, which, much to my husband's dismay, I have on occasion done. The produce, like a choir, hums backup for the flowers by adding its own riotous art-glass venue: lemons, oranges, asparagus, radishes, apples, carrots, kale, and grapefruit all sing along while the old lady boogies in aisle three.

No doubt about it—nothing shouts stained glass profusion like a garden, even an already harvested one at Kroger's. And if you take note, most stained glass designs contain flowers. Les made me a stained glass lamp shade designed with water lilies vining around the glass. I also have large patio stones into which he has set stained glass designs, and all of them contain something in blossom. I mean, who doesn't want flowers that bloom all year long strewn on her path? I rest my case.

On through the watching of that early birth
When, just as the soil tarnishes with weed,
The sturdy seedling with arched body comes
Shouldering its ways and shedding the earth crumbs.
(Robert Frost, from "Putting in the Seed")

I've had gardens of varying sizes throughout my married life, from a teacup of ivy on my kitchen sill, to a pot of geraniums on our stoop, to a row of blossoms running alongside our home, to a backyard crammed full of stemmed beauties. I tend to be an eclectic gardener in that I encourage a little disorderly conduct in my patches. I'm not a sculpted garden architect, but I do appreciate tidy designs from afar. Give me instead bed-head clusters of butterfly bushes, sweet Williams, hollyhocks, nasturtiums, lavender, snapdragons, day lilies, and sprays of roses. Add to that a side yard full of cutting flowers, like hydrangeas, Queen Anne's Lace, sweet peas, bells of Ireland, black-eyed Susans, peonies, pansies, bachelor buttons, cornflowers, Veronicas, and dill. Don't forget a few shade plants, like impatiens, lily-of-the-valley, and violets, to brighten corners. Oh, yes, and one must have sun-drenched trellises full of morning glories and clematis. No doubt about it, a chubby garden, like radiant stained glass windows, makes me a happy girl.

I don't think anything is more therapeutic for me than gathering an armload of flowers from the yard, arranging them in a vase, and then discovering just the right place to show them off. That is, after dusting off the spiders and ants, shooing off the bees, and trimming the contrary stems. Oh, what aggravating things the fall of humanity did to the garden.

Since I'm new to Tennessee, I'm still learning about the soil and growing season, so I haven't done much yet to flower-fy my surroundings. Our two-story home is draped in trees shading our front yard, which limits our flower choices there. Our back-yard mostly is cement, but the wooden fence offers opportunity for hanging baskets, and I envision the side yard off the kitchen loaded with herbs.

> When weeding, the best way to make sure you are removing a weed and not a valuable plant is to pull on it. If it comes out of the ground easily, it is a valuable plant.
>
> —AUTHOR UNKNOWN

Our lot is small, which matches our declining energy. Once acreage was exciting to us; today it's downright exhausting. We would rather porch-sit and watch neighbors with large yards do the landscaping while we rock and applaud youthful vigor.

Although I do have to have some blossoms and leafy wonders close by for my mental health. Last fall that came in the form of hanging baskets on the front porch, but this year I want to expand . . . and if that increase isn't enough, maybe I'll climb over yonder neighbor's fence and dig awhile just for old times' sake.

What causes us to feel drawn to gardens? The beauty? The fragrances? The color? The variety? The serenity? How about all of the above and more? Much more.

In a visit to a women's prison, my companion first led me to a prayer garden that was tended by nuns. She said it was a good place to quiet our hearts before we entered the emotional chaos of the prison. Even though it was a desert garden, which is very different from a Michigan or Tennessee garden, the same serenity wrapped around my heart as I sat clustered in yellow poppies and purple owl clover.

In monastic gardens during medieval times, monks, like the nuns we visited, nurtured gardens for food, medicine, and the labor it afforded their disciplined lifestyle. Often the garden was their place of prayer. Frequently the monks ran infirmaries on their grounds to tend to the ill in their own community and townsfolk nearby. Many of the cures were literally rooted in their flower beds. They used chamomile for abrasions, respiratory issues, and arthritis; hollyhocks for fevers, sore throats, and as a laxative. Feverfew, a beautiful, white-petaled flower with a yellow-green center, was used for headaches and psoriasis; lemon balm, a plant with small, white flowers, has lemony leaves used for teas and aids those with colds and flu.

From the beginning gardens were meant to be home.

Perhaps that's why we long to be in them—for their refuge, shade, privacy, and peace. My heart stills when I sit in the midst of lavender and roses. The heady fragrance and gentle beauty feeds a need inside me that I can't even express. To witness a butterfly when it settles in on a delicate petal and then flutters away is to see poetry take wing. Or to watch a portly bumblebee crawl upside down inside a flower as if it's a pub and come out staggering, hardly able to flit its way home, causes me to giggle.

When my hubby starts a stained glass project, he buys a pattern that looks like a preliminary garden sketch. It's full of sections carefully subdivided and numbered. He then cuts out glass shapes and "plants" them on the pattern. He then "waters" with foil and solder, and once they're in place, he "transplants" them to a window to allow the sunshine to do the rest.

Speaking of the sun, years ago I had a bed of spindly pansies in my yard that weren't getting enough sunlight; so I dug them up in clumps and repositioned them. They initially acted as if they had lost their best friend. Their heads hung, the stems were unable to stand; they looked forlorn. Then I gave them a good soaking and let the sun do the rest. Soon their little faces were heavenward, drinking in the rays, their roots replenished, and every stem stood tall. Their happy faces reminded me of kindergartners at recess, full of dreams and wonder.

As Les and I in the last year were transplanted from our birth state of Michigan to our current home in Tennessee, we at times have felt like a clump of pansies that had been dug up and replanted in someone else's yard. At first it was easy to pick us out in the "garden" of our neighborhood . . . we were the ones who weren't quite rooted and looked bewildered in this fresh plot. But as the months have gone on, we're finding our way around, learning our neighbors, and we are feeling more at home in our surroundings. Faces heavenward, we've been reassured by the Lord of his presence, and we are giggly with gratitude.

Change is transitional. Even if it's your dream come true. Change initially tilts our center.

Here are things we've found helpful while transitioning into and through a significant change.

- Plant seeds of hope by expecting the best. Don't have ridiculous expectations, but do look for God's hand at work wherever you are . . . because it is.

  "The earth is the LORD's, and everything in it, the world, and all who live in it." (Psalm 24:1 NIV)

- Weed out regret. Once you make your decision to plow a certain field (new job, home, school, etc.), don't second-guess yourself. You will only stir up yellow jackets of insecurity. Keep tabs on what's buzzing around in your mind. Shoo off thoughts that keep you negative and sad. Deliberately lift your pansy face heavenward.

"Be anxious for nothing, but in everything by prayer and supplication with thanksgiving let your requests be made known to God. And the peace of God, which surpasses all comprehension, will guard your hearts and minds in Christ Jesus." (Philippians 4:6–7)

- Water your mind and words generously with gratitude. Find as many things as you can each day to be thankful for . . . like the way the sunlight climbs up your front steps and splays stained glass patterns across your front door; the way doves hover near your window and coo soft sounds of love; the way tulips surprised you and blossom behind your garage next to the trash bin. Then there's the smell of fresh coffee, new leather, old lavender. Or what about a kitten's warm purr, a puppy's eager greeting, a gaggle of geese honking their way home?

  Change is enhanced by a grateful heart. Be a detective and go in search of your happy. Make a list of things that bring the sunshine back into your patch.

  "Rejoice in the Lord always; again I will say, rejoice!" (Philippians 4:4)

- Remember, rooting takes both time and tilling. One part, the tilling, is up to us; the other, time, we have to wait on. Like spring. Just about the time you want to give up and believe the lie that winter will never leave, a petite grape hyacinth sprouts up with determination, pleading the cause of hope eternal.

> *Wait for the Lord;*
> *Be strong and let your heart take courage;*
> *Yes, wait for the Lord.*
>
> (PSALM 27:14)

Plant seeds of hope.
Weed out regrets.
Water generously.
Remember it will take tilling and time.

Yep, becoming a garden means you will crawl in the dirt, lie dormant through some seasons, be resurrected in the spring, and blossom till the freeze comes. The circle of life.

Scripture starts with a garden and ends with one; so you know they are important for this life and the next. When I picked a life verse more than thirty-five years ago, it was Psalm 1:2–3. This is *The Message* version:

> *Instead you thrill to God's Word,*
> *you chew on Scripture day and night.*
> *You're a tree replanted in Eden,*
> *bearing fresh fruit every month,*

Never dropping a leaf,
always in blossom.

And its companion verse in Jeremiah 17:7–8 (also from *The Message*):

But blessed is the man who trusts me, God,
the woman who sticks with God.
They're like trees replanted in Eden,
putting down roots near the rivers—
Never a worry through the hottest of summers,
never dropping a leaf,
Serene and calm through droughts,
bearing fresh fruit every season.

My prayer is that I would remain fruitful all the days of my life. Do you have a life verse? Choose one that represents the desire of your heart. God will honor that.

The Art Gallery ———————————————

Memorial: The Survivor Tree, which is an elm more than ninety years old, stands rooted on the land designated as the Outdoor Symbolic Memorial—site of the Oklahoma City bombing. On April 19, 1995, 168 people died. The outdoor site was designed as a place of remembrance and reflection.

From above it looks like an English garden with its glass-like reflecting pool, its meticulously cared-for flowers and nut-bearing trees that depict the survivors and the rescuers, and the lit "garden of chairs" that commemorates each person who died. The chairs are positioned in nine rows, and from above appear to grow out of the land. Visiting the garden is a solemn, sobering, and sacred experience. You sense the devastation of loss followed by the determination of hope.

Scripture:

Oh, visit the earth,
ask her to join the dance!
Deck her out in spring showers,
fill the God-River with living water.
Paint the wheat fields golden.
Creation was made for this!
Drench the plowed fields,
soak the dirt clods
With rainfall as harrow and rake
bring her to blossom and fruit.
Snow-crown the peaks with splendor,
scatter rose petals down your paths,
All through the wild meadows, rose petals.
Set the hills to dancing,
Dress the canyon walls with live sheep,

a drape of flax across the valleys.
Let them shout, and shout, and shout!
Oh, oh, let them sing!

(PSALM 65:9–13 MSG)

Chapter 12

Stained Glass
Rock of Ages

The older I get, the madder my hair is at me. My hair was once thick, curly, and sanguine, similar to a Chia Pet. Now my hair is a thin scramble of melancholy cowlicks. Don't you hate the term *cowlicks* for something that sits atop your head? Sounds like a herd of bovine has been slobbering on me. As much as I appreciate nature, I'm definitely opposed to slobber.

I once had such a wad of frizz atop my head that it must have covered all the sticky-outie parts, but now my hair is a thin clump of slathered tumbleweed. Its true nature is unpredictable; all twelve hairs on my head just said, "Amen." I daily use five styling products just to point my hair in the right direction. Yes, five. Every morning I'm startled by my hair's unruly behavior.

> Time may be a great healer, but it's a lousy beautician.
>
> —AUTHOR UNKNOWN

I really don't mind my age, but I do find the "draperies" that come with it troubling. It's not easy to gather up all that loose material and harness things in place every day. The task is wearisome, but someone has to do it, if for no other reason than to protect the environment.

And that's not all . . .

I could have a garage sale for chins. Where did they all come from? Relatives? Gee, thanks. I would rather they left me their sterling. Really, I wish they had retrieved a few of these, uh, baggies. They get in my way. I tried wrapping them in scarves, but then I looked like an ancient tortoise trying to get her head out of a shell. Besides, it's embarrassing when a couple of the chins suddenly pop out like a jill-in-the-box or some such thing. I considered a chin strap, but then I realized if I started to strap up everything that's sagging, I'd end up looking like a ball of twine.

I know there are benefits to aging, but they keep slipping my mind. Speaking of which, once my brain had tidy card files like a Dewey decimal system at the library; now it's more like a lottery. No one knows what might come out or if it will be fully clothed and in its right mind.

But all kidding . . . ahem . . . aside . . .

There are lovely parts to aging. Honest. Even the relaxed skin takes me back to my grandmother. I remember loving to trace her purple-ribboned veins in her soft hands and to touch her frail arms with their lovely transparency. I was careful lest the skin tear. I always was surprised by the strength in her hands, as if she was determined to hang on to life's vigor as long as she could. And she did. When Mamaw died at the age of ninety-seven, her mind was still as crisp as the starched ruffles on her kitchen curtains.

Mamaw's hair thinned through the years, and she had adapted her style to fit the change. A few hand fluffs to her cotton candy, purply red hair, and she was good to go. She was more concerned with praying for her sick neighbor and studying her Sunday school lesson than in creating an impressive hairdo. On Sunday-go-to-meeting day, Mamaw would sport a hat, usually red. She would carry her black "pocketbook," always making sure she had a hankie and gloves (freshly laundered). Being a lady was Mamaw's priority along with being prompt. Her Bible, the size of Grant's tomb, was carried proudly.

I understand why folks steam dry their wrinkles and take tucks to hike things up hither and yon, but I sure appreciate the au naturel woman who gives me permission to live with myself and then demonstrates how it's done. I don't recall my mamaw whining about her age;

> Some people, no matter how old they get, never lose their beauty—they merely move it from their faces into their hearts.
>
> —MARTIN BUXBAUM

in fact, she wore it like a trophy. When you asked her how old she was, she would stand straighter, as if she were about to announce the winner for the Kentucky Derby, and with a gleam in her eye, she would tell you. Then she would wait for your response and applause. I remember how inflated Mamaw's joy became when she was recognized as the oldest member at her church.

Today's culture doesn't seem to view old as gold . . . hmm, this could have international implications.

My friends Luci Swindoll and Marilyn Meberg put verve and nerve into aging. They give it a fresh slant. Their stained glass windows are highlighted with glitter. Full of fun and optimism, they make the years dance. While they are my seniors, I feel as if Junior (that would be me) is catching up to their candle count. I appreciate that, even though they are very different from each other in some ways, they pave the yellow brick path ahead with a shared sense of high-stepping style. They are active world travelers, eager learners, gifted conversationalists, art connoisseurs, and wacky women from the get-go.

When I want to sit down and pout about lost years or what might happen in the future regarding physical and mental limitations, I think how these girls chase rainbows at the drop of a flag, like at the Indy 500. That inspires me to rev up and floor it into a new adventure. Like cooking school . . .

Yep, I went to a four-hour cooking school last week (way out of my comfort zone) to learn how to cook fish. And I attended with witnesses. Nervy. My hubby and our friends Steve and Karen Anderson made up our team of four, along with about eight others in the class, whom we didn't know.

We learned how to salt-bake a fish with the head and tail still on. The sea creature was looking right at us when we patted it down. We packed it in two pounds of coarse kosher salt, and when it came out of the oven, we cracked open the casement with a mallet—my favorite part. Then we lifted the backbone out, taking all the other bones with it (ha!). We also fixed apple-chip smoked salmon (actually we didn't smoke; the smoker did the puffing), potato-crusted striped bass with lemon beurre blanc, prosciutto-wrapped grouper, and grilled ahi on rosemary skewers. But the best part was . . . we ate it all. I felt very international.

You might be saying, "C'mon, Patsy, you can take a bigger risk than cooking." But then you've never eaten my cooking. But you're right; I have taken riskier moves. Recently I came across a snapshot that I took of a family of elephants while I was dangling over the side of a hot air balloon in Tanzania. How's that for risky?

Not long before that trip, if anyone had told me I would go to Africa or ride in a hot air balloon, I wouldn't have believed it. Africa wasn't on my bucket list. It makes me *pail* just thinking of it. Get it? Bucket . . . pail. Never mind. The point is I don't like long trips, and I don't do heights. Well, I didn't. But now I have a bragging list, and Africa is right at the top.

Beware, though. You can lose your heart to that mysterious land and its resilient people. Like sentinels, the acacias stand in a sea of endless land that runs up distant hills into dusty clouds. Herds of migrating zebras as far as the eye can see stripe the dry land as they make their way to water. Lone hyenas with bony shoulder blades heckle and sulk a distance away. Giraffes sway and reach the treetops' most tender leaves. Vegetarians, I suspect. And then there are the lions . . . hello.

Oh, Africa, how could I have known you would stay inside me like a cherished song? It's as if I had only known ballads, and then somebody introduced me to jazz: a thrilling, heart-moving world of sights and sounds swaying with the pulse of its people. The sunsets explode across the horizon, encircling this wild, winsome land in stained glass wonder.

And to think I almost didn't go because it was outside my experience. Live outside the lines of your list. Be international . . . at least in heart. Don't miss the adventure God has for you!

I keep pushing myself to tiptoe beyond the boundaries of my safety net. That way I can freshen my brain cells to think in new directions. My tendency is to stay with a few tried-and-true recipes, to walk home on a known path, and to wear the same slippers until they corrode on my feet and have to be scraped off. But my tendency doesn't have to be my reality; so move over, Julia—here comes another contender . . . well, then again, maybe not. I may never compete with the Iron Chefs, but I can fortify my brain and enjoy the years I have left with a little pizzazz and a lot of joy.

> When it comes to staying young, a mind-lift beats a face-lift any day.
>
> —MARTY BUCELLA

I may never return to Africa, but I will always hold close the memories, sights, and smells. I can close my eyes right now and feel the sun's warmth, hear the children's laughter, see the women's kind faces, and hear the animals' calls in the night.

One thing I've learned after circling the block of life at breakneck speed is that you need a sense of humor to survive aging—actually, to survive life. Otherwise a case of ornery can seize you, and you'll break out in cranky. And that's never cute on anyone.

Years ago I met an older woman at the hospital where we were both patients for minor issues. She was tall, held herself very properly, and had a twinkle in her eye that was winsome. It turned out she was legally blind, but she was astute and seldom required assistance at anything she did. Her hearing was fine-tuned, and she knew the sound of my step. I only knew her for a few days, and that was forty years ago. But I've never forgotten her humor, optimism, and faith. I left the hospital before her, and when I returned to see her, I was told that a nurse went in to check on her one morning, and she was asleep in the Lord. No struggle. No sign of pain or panic. Just peace. Sweet peace.

Jan Lievens, a portrait painter from the Netherlands in the 1600s, was a child prodigy. He produced works that became classics by the time he was fourteen. (At fourteen, I still was playing with paper dolls and watching *The Lone Ranger*.) He and his friend Rembrandt shared a studio in their teenage years.

Even though Lievens chose diverse subjects for his paintings, I noticed many were of the elderly. The one that caught my eye is entitled *Portrait of the Artist's Mother*. The aging woman is leaning over her large lap Bible in rapt attention. I have the sense she is

> It's important to have a twinkle in your wrinkle.
>
> —AUTHOR UNKNOWN

reading something that she has read many times before, but it still stirs her heart. She is wearing pince-nez (squeeze-on spectacles with no temple pieces) and leans into the words so as not to miss one. A swath of light across the pages illuminates the text, or perhaps the text is illuminating her. The woman's mouth is parted, making me think that as she reads she forms the words on her lips in a whisper—a common habit of the elderly (me) to help them (me) focus. Ah, but sometimes our mouths are agape so we might taste again the wine of Christ's love.

> When grace is joined with wrinkles, it is adorable. There is an unspeakable dawn in happy old age.
>
> —VICTOR HUGO

As I grow older, I notice that I seek the shelter of silence more and more. In years gone by, I would flip on the television or music when I was alone. But now, given the option, I turn off everything. It allows the quiet to settle inside my ruffled places, inside the voices of the day and hushes them, and inside the demands of my tomorrows. I need the quiet to balance the frenetic in my life. I need the quiet to discern Christ's voice from all the others.

Sometimes Christ's voice to me is a waterfall, and I couldn't miss it on the freeway during rush hour, but usually it's a soft rain, a gentle breeze, or even a whisper, and I must lean in to hear.

The quiet gives me opportunity to sort myself out in God's presence. That's when I stop any pretending and excusing. The stillness gives me space for confession and petitions. I open the stained glass window of my soul. My heart finds centeredness in God's grace.

The Art Gallery ―――――――――――――――――

Stained Glass: Near the Rotunda of the Capitol building in Washington, DC, a prayer room features a stained glass window. In the center of the window is George Washington kneeling in prayer with the verse "Preserve me, O God: for in thee do I put my trust" (Psalm 16:1 KJV) inscribed in the stained glass surrounding the prayerful president. This room is for representatives and senators to seek God's counsel and to sort their thoughts. We can see it online (Google "congressional prayer room"), but the room isn't open for tours. I'm grateful to know it's there and that the "father of our country" is shown in a contrite position, acknowledging his need of God to guide our young country.

Museum: *The National Gallery, Washington, DC.* In 1840 American painter Thomas Cole created an allegory of life in four paintings. Each painting is set in a boat, and the paintings begin with a young child whose guardian angel is at the helm. Next the child is a young man who has taken over steering the boat and heads toward a castle in the sky. In the third picture he is a man making his way through life's rough waters, and finally he is an old man headed across the waters to eternity with the angel once again at the helm. The surrounding landscape changes in each picture to help tell the story, as does the direction of the boat in the water. What doesn't change is the angel's presence. I like that. I need to know I'm companioned and my boat is steered.

Looking back, life unfolds at warp speed. We're amazed when we browse through pictures and wonder where time went. Like a moth it flitted through the soft glow of a porch light and then disappeared into the night. Even more startling is to realize we are nearing the final boat ride (speaking for myself, of course). My childhood is done; my youth is over; my young adult life is past; so that puts me in frame four.

Perhaps Cole should have painted a fifth frame and allowed the fourth to be a transitional voyager before the old-age boat. You know, one in which the traveler helps the angel to steer.

Music: "Legacy," Nichole Nordeman. If you're unfamiliar with Nichole's work, rush to iTunes and load up on her work and words; they will change your life. This woman's heart well is deep, her words are lush, and her voice is delicate and rich. She is an old soul in a young body with something to say.

Poems: "Ripening" by Wendell Berry.

> *Lives of great men all remind us*
> *We can make our lives sublime,*
> *And, departing, leave behind us*
> *Footprints on the sand of time.*

(HENRY WADSWORTH LONGFELLOW, FROM "A PSALM OF LIFE")

Stained Glass: A full-fledged glass sort of legacy hangs in the Lincoln Cathedral in Lincolnshire, England. Some describe the stained glass windows, when lit, as shining like a lighthouse over a sea of undulating fields and moors. Ancient footprints of light, so to speak. The first cathedral on the land was completed in 1092, but much of it was destroyed by an earthquake in 1185. It was rebuilt between 1192 and 1235. Yet 70 percent of the glass in the cathedral is original. Imagine that. Go to www.lincolncathedral.com to read the history and to view the building and windows. Don't miss the Rose Window. It's spectacular.

Scripture: "Rise in the presence of the aged, show respect for the elderly and revere your God. I am the LORD." (Leviticus 19:32 NIV)

> *The silver-haired head is a crown of glory,*
> *If it is found in the way of righteousness.*
>
> (PROVERBS 16:31 NKJV)

> *The righteous shall flourish like a palm tree,*
> *He shall grow like a cedar in Lebanon.*
> *Those who are planted in the house of the LORD*
> *Shall flourish in the courts of our God.*
> *They shall still bear fruit in old age;*
> *They shall be fresh and flourishing.*
>
> (PSALM 92:12–14 NKJV)

Video: Check out the amazing video of a resurrection mural by Ron DiCianni, with the artist explaining the choices he made in painting it. It's a trip through Scripture. Go to http://www.cbn.com. Then type into the search box "resurrection mural."

Chapter 13

Stained Glass Redemption

The small but stately church sits proudly in our town. She owns her corner well, with her history-laden turret bruised by a Civil War cannonball and her stained glass windows designed by Tiffany himself. She's got style.

I attended Easter services there, and the experience was more than I could have imagined. The structure has been lovingly cared for, which has resulted in a cathedral confidence that you sense as you enter the diminutive sanctuary. The windows, stained with stories of our faith, are lovely reminders of what matters: the risen Christ, the Good Shepherd, and the soon-coming King. I noted that the stained glass windows, rather than causing a person to look out, caused one to look in. The windows stirred congregants to consider their own pieced-together lives, their own redeemed stories.

The pews were full of eager participants, shoulder to shoulder. The anticipation of the service's beginning was palpable; children wiggled, adults thumped their hymnals, choir members craned their necks. The church choir was small, but their sound was full, one of the finest chorales I have heard. I didn't dare breathe lest I miss one glorious note. The service was short, joyful, and celebratory. At the close, bells rang out, trumpets sounded, a golden cross entwined in lilies was lifted, and someone proclaimed, "He's alive! He's alive! Christ is alive!"

Then people spilled down the steps, which were staggered with pots of tall lilies, and into the street, where the trees' boughs were heavy with blossoms. As folks greeted one another, I stood in a pool of sunlight and thought the scene was like a dream. I felt renewed. My prayer was, "Oh, that Easter might come in this manner all year round." We were designed to be interactive in our faith, in the telling of our stories, and in the proclaiming of Christ's.

Just as stained windows require ongoing repair and protection through the years, so do we. But you knew that. Life is a strong teacher of such things. But I have to repeat to myself some truths again and again or they slip my mind. My busy-about-many-things lifestyle can cause me to buzz right past my needs until I start to shard. Then, stopped in my tracks, this truth comes to me: "Oh, yes, I need to be still for repairs." To the degree I respond, I gain a healthier perspective.

I'm not sure how I get drawn into the fray of life; yet before I know it, I'm taking on too much, overextending my measures of strength, talking too much, blaming, eating too much too often, which then leaves me calorie-laden and cantankerous.

Life seems to come in spurts, and as I jog from one spurt to the next, I guess I've become a bona fide spurt chaser. I want more.

But that's not how I want to flip over the calendar days I have left. I want the etching on my window to be a story highlighted with intention, peace, joy, and love. All of which take availability to God's Spirit as he guides, leads, transforms, and empowers.

I just read a few great blog posts in which folks listed how to wake up earlier: drink water upon rising, put the alarm clock across the room, exercise immediately; then sit quietly to collect your thoughts, eat strategically, and pet a pet. I believe everything they said, and when I do rise up early after a good night's rest, I'm glad I made the effort. But getting up at daybreak and moving body parts rapidly sounds dangerous. As far as "eat strategically," I've never eaten a strategy and wouldn't know how to prepare it without a recipe. I don't own a pet, but I enjoy scratching behind my hubby's ears. Does that count? Dawn will never be easy for me; my internal Big Ben isn't programmed for early entrances. I'm more your final-curtain-call girl.

> Guard well your spare moments. They are like uncut diamonds. Discard them, and their value will never be known. Improve them, and they will become the brightest gems in a useful life.
>
> —RALPH WALDO EMERSON

This past Christmas my daughter-in-law, Danya, gave me a darling nightshirt that reads, "Morning and me are not compatible." She thought it was funny. I thought it made perfect sense. Ah, but here's what makes me want to go against my compatibility tendencies—the clock is literally ticking. I can hear it, and I have to be about my Father's business.

I've observed that the components in a richly textured existence are seldom natural. They tend to go against the grain of humanity. It's part of the buffing used to soften sharp edges.

When I began speaking for women's groups, the events were in my home state and Les or my friend Rose would drive me. Then I received out-of-state invitations, which made it trickier to plan road trips; yet somehow we did it. But when I was invited to California, that meant I would have to fly—a feat I was reserving for glory, when I would sprout wings and be in charge of my own landing gear.

> Our Lord needs from us neither great deeds nor profound thoughts. Neither intelligence nor talents. He cherishes simplicity.
>
> —SAINT THERESE OF LISIEUX

Here's what I learned: when my desire to go became greater than my fear of airplanes, I boarded. True, my knees ricocheted off each other so hard they were bruised, but I did it. Airplanes and I weren't naturally compatible. That was thirty-five years ago. I now have accrued more than two million miles on one airline and almost that many on another one. I didn't know on that first flight it would become a way of life for me, or I might have run back home to the safety of my insecurity. But if I was going to do what God had called me to, that fear had to be buffed out of my story.

The path ahead is getting shorter, and I want my last steps

to matter. I know you do as well. I don't want fear to hamper me from taking shaky steps forward, and I certainly don't want to sleep through life participation. I realize I can't afford to panic now. I've come too far. So instead, I take refuge in the truth that Jesus is the author and finisher of our faith (Hebrews 12:2). Emphasis for me now rests on *finisher*.

My mind has lost some of its snappy edge; my balance in unexpected moments borders on tipsy; and my memory has been peppered with buckshot. So I need a finisher; otherwise, I would be afraid of the days ahead.

I saw a quote on Twitter recently that read, "The bridge between panic and peace is prayer." So I'm using my extra morning time, since I'm rising up a tad earlier these days, to cross that bridge to peace.

As I write, I'm recovering from pneumonia. I've been housebound far too long for my excitable personality. So yesterday I dragged a chair into my driveway where there was a patch of sunshine, sat down, and with my face tilted toward the sun, I had my prayer time. I'm sure the neighbors thought they had an elderly escapee loose since I was donned in nightclothes and coiffed in bed-head. For me, though, the time in God's spotlight was a sweet bridging from my cabin fever to finding the still waters within as I sat in Christ's presence.

Peace offers such a sacred perspective. Unruffled behavior. Quiet confidence. Calm heart. Untroubled mind. Tranquil outlook. Aren't you drawn to people with a serene center who have the space and grace to receive others? I am.

For those of us given to busyness and control, I think the word *purposed* conjures up images that include organized productivity, but *simplicity* takes us to a calmer, saner, uncluttered, less-driven place. Certainly one of order, but beyond the order is the settled issues of the heart . . . like who is actually in charge.

> For me, prayer is an upward leap of the heart . . . a cry of gratitude and love which I utter from the depths of sorrow as well as from the heights of joy. It has a supernatural grandeur which expands the soul and unites it with God.
>
> —SAINT THERESE OF LISIEUX

Supernatural grandeur expands our souls and helps us throughout the day to live not in glass-breaking tension but in tiptoe perspective. It's the place where, in our "upward leap of the heart," we see beyond the fray to the Father who does all things well.

I want to be like the stately church in my hometown. I want to own my corner well, including my history-laden bruises. I want cathedral confidence that comes when my diminutive story is colored with the risen Christ, the Good Shepherd, and the soon-coming King. May the songs within us be breathtaking, and may our lives clearly proclaim, "He's alive! He's alive! Christ is alive!"

About the Author

Patsy Clairmont's quick wit and depth of biblical knowledge combine in a powerful pint-size package. She will help you laugh God's truths right into your heart. Patsy's mission to provide humor and hope for healing comes from her own struggles. God pulled together the emotionally fragmented pieces of her life, not only to free her but also to serve as a reminder that imperfect, *cracked* Christians are God's specialty.

A recovering agoraphobic, Patsy speaks to women from all walks of life: "Take a deep breath and pop a dark-chocolate bonbon; we girls are in this together." As a result of her appearances at Women of Faith, which she has been a part of since its inception, Patsy addresses tens of thousands of women each month. She has also written more than twenty-four books, including *Catching Fireflies*, *All Cracked Up*, and *I Grew Up Little*, in addition to contributing to numerous Women of Faith multiauthor books.

Patsy loves a rainy day, a good book, and a deep cushioned chair. Given a day off, she shops, decorates, solves the world's problems with a friend over lunch, and hugs the stuffing out of her two grandsons, Justin and Noah. She also avoids numbers, celebrates words, and eats entirely too many chocolate chip cookies. Patsy and her husband of forty-nine years, Les, live in Tennessee. They have two sons, Marty and Jason; a daughter-in-law, Danya; and a granddog, Cody, who jumps higher than Patsy is tall.

www.patsyclairmont.com

Now that you've read her words on the page . . .

You'll love hearing Patsy tell her stories in her own inimitable way, live and in person. But that's not all! At a Women of Faith event, you'll also hear from other fabulous speakers, enjoy wonderful music, and experience a time of connection—with other women and with God.

"I just wanted to personally thank all of you for all of the inspirational stories and music . . . just what so many of us needed. It is nice to know that you aren't the only one that has been broken and that God is the only one that can put us back together." Brandy C.

Hear Patsy (and friends) in person at Women of Faith!

Find dates, locations, talent lineup, and registration information at womenoffaith.com or call 888.49.FAITH (888.493.2484) for details or to register by phone.

Register Today!